THE MODERN KU KLUX KLAN

THE MODERN
KU KLUX KLAN

BY

HENRY P. FRY

BOSTON
SMALL, MAYNARD & COMPANY
PUBLISHERS

PREFACE

IT seems strange that, in narrating events and analyzing an organization existing in the United States of America in the year 1921, the most appropriate introduction to the subject consists of a few pages from the history of Germany during the Middle Ages. There existed in mediæval Germany a secret organization, which, in its highest stage of development is said to have numbered over 200,000 members — the *Vehmgericht,* or secret tribunal. Its origin is clouded in obscurity, some authorities claiming that the system was first founded by Charlemagne, while others say that it was handed down from the most remote pre-historic Germans, but is understood generally to have first appeared in the year 1180 in Westphalia, after which it scattered all over Germany.

Its head was the Emperor, assisted by the nobles of his court, and with them men of all ranks, associated together for the formation of "free courts," to try persons accused of crimes against persons and property. The members of the organization were known as "*Wissende,*" or initiated ones. They were bound by solemn oaths not to reveal the circumstances of a trial or the sentence imposed on the offender if found guilty; and in order to become one of the brother-

hood the applicant was required to be of good
character, and have two sureties who were
already "free judges." A ceremony of initiation, usually held in some out-of-the-way place,
inducted the outsider into the organization, and
thereafter, he was required under his solemn
oath never to reveal the fact that he was a
member of the brotherhood. The initiated ones
recognized each other by signs.

The *Vehmgericht* could be summoned at any
time and place, in private buildings, in the
forests, in caves, or in the open fields; they were
occasionally held publicly, but usually they
were closed against all but the initiated and the
accused person. The Emperor, or, in his absence,
the count or noble of highest dignity presided,
and if any uninitiated person intruded, he was
immediately put to death. The secret tribunal
met when necessary and received complaints,
to answer which they assumed the right to
summon any one in Germany. Ordinarily, the
accused was arrested and held by his captors
for the secret trial, but if he had not been
arrested, he was summoned to appear by fas-
tening on his door or gateway the summons of
the dreaded court, which usually had enclosed
in it a small coin. If he failed to appear or send
a messenger, he was condemned, as despising
the jurisdiction of the Holy *Vehmgericht*, and
once condemned there was little chance of his
life while he remained in Germany.

The condemnation of an offender by a

Vehmic Court was known to the whole brotherhood in a short time; and even if it were the father, brother, or son of one of the initiated who was condemned, he not only might not warn him of his danger, but was bound to aid in putting him to death under penalty of losing his own life.

The death penalty, the usual decree of the court, was generally inflicted by hanging. When executed the victim was hanged to the nearest tree, nothing of value which he might have about him being removed, and a knife was thrust into the ground as a token that the deed had been committed by order of the brotherhood.

The *Vehmgericht*, although an irresponsible tribunal possessing this extensive and dreadful authority, became a power so formidable that Charles IV, in 1371, stipulated for its official recognition. Exercising its despotic dominion under such obligations of severity, the brotherhood, however, in 1461, incurred the hostility of those who feared to become its victims, as well as those who saw in it an engine capable of terrible oppression, and an association was formed to resist it. The result was that, in 1495, Maximilian I established a new criminal code, materially weakening the secret tribunals. Secret trials are said to have been held as late as 1811, although the brotherhood ceased to excite terror or exert any considerable influence before the close of the seventeenth century.

In the year 1914 the prosaic American people,

self-satisfied in a national peace and prosperity
that superficially appeared to be a permanent
condition, were suddenly awakened to find
themselves spectators of the great drama staged
by Emperor William Hohenzollern, who suddenly plunged all Europe into the throes of a
Napoleonic war.

In the year 1915 another "Emperor"— this
time an American — conceived a scheme, which,
instead of reversing time merely for one hundred years, would take the nation back to the
days of German mediævalism — back to the
Vehmgericht, the secret tribunal and the days of
irresponsible government clandestinely administered.

This monstrosity, conceived in a brain that
must have been either inanely visionary or
superlatively cunning, has been let loose in the
land, where for the past twelve months, it has
been vigorously propagated by a highly organized, highly industrious, and highly paid force
of experienced and trained propagandists. Its
appeal is to group hatred and group prejudice; its
organization, which is strictly secret, has, in
some of its units, already followed the methods
of the *Vehmgericht;* the title of its "wizard"
comes from the "*Wissende*" or initiated of the
German brotherhood; its structure is military;
its aims are political; and, openly calling itself
the "Invisible Empire," it is an autocracy in
government, ruled by an "Emperor" who has
placed himself on the throne for life.

It was my privilege to have been a member — one of the *"Wissende"* — in this secret movement, which is legally known as the Knights of the Ku Klux Klan; and I had the opportunity of investigating it from the inside, observing its direful potentialities.

When I became thorough acquainted with the thing, I withdrew from it, as I felt that it was dangerous, vicious and absolutely out of place in the American Republic. I therefore decided to expose it, and to make the "Invisible Empire" visible to the people of the United States. To accomplish this desired end, I turned over to the *New York World* all of the information I possessed; and that great newspaper, after three months of nation-wide investigation, told the people the truth about Ku Kluxism, and the "Invisible Empire."

Supplementary to the work of the *New York World*, I offer this book, which consists largely of articles written as an investigator for that newspaper, many of which were used as a basis for its investigations. To the *World* belongs all the credit for this exposure and investigation, and when the American people fully understand and thoroughly realize what Ku Kluxism means, they will, of course, feel obligated to the *World* for its work in undertaking and carrying out the task of eliminating this un-American movement from this country.

Personally, I wish to express my deep appreciation to Mr. Herbert B. Swope, Executive

Editor, Mr. William P. Beazell, Assistant Managing Editor, and Mr. Rowland Thomas, of the *New York World*, both for having taken hold of the matter and so ably handling it, and also for their many acts of courtesy shown to me while the work was in progress.

HENRY P. FRY.

TABLE OF CONTENTS

THE MODERN KU KLUX KLAN

CHAPTER I

INTRODUCTION

IF the psychologist, looking over the diversified and conflicting interests and classes of the American people, attempted to find a common state of mind, he would probably discover one thing that applies to all American men, without regard to "race, color, or previous condition of servitude." He would learn that there is a common American trait possessed by the white man and the negro, the Jew and the Gentile, the Catholic and the Protestant, the native and the foreign-born — in fact by every conceivable group of the males of the United States.

They are all "joiners"!

One has to search far and wide for an American who does not "belong" to some sort of organization, and who would not, under proper circumstances, join another.

I am a joiner-by-birth.

My joining developed at the early age of ten, when I organized a secret society among the boys at school. We had an awful oath to which

1

we swore, and in imitation of Huckleberry Finn and Tom Sawyer, sealed it with our blood. We had no fees or dues, but each boy was required to contribute a copy of *Nick Carter* or *Diamond Dick* or *Old Cap Collier*. The organization survived a brief period and was then ruthlessly destroyed by an irate parent who disapproved of its intellectual standards.

I had scarcely reached the age of twenty-one and started life in Chattanooga as a newspaper reporter, when I took up seriously the habit of joining fraternal orders. In five years I had taken degrees in practically every one to which I was eligible. I became a Mason, a Knight of Pythias, an Odd Fellow, a Red Man, a member of the Junior Order United American Mechanics, of the Royal Arcanum, of the Woodmen, an Elk, an Eagle, an Owl, and an associate member of the Theatrical Mechanics Association.

The last "order" I joined was the Knights of the Ku Klux Klan.

I went into this one partly because I was a joiner and was curious to see what it was all about, but principally because I thought it was a fraternal order which was actually a revival of the original Ku Klux Klan which played so important a part in the history of the South during the days of the Reconstruction. That old organization has always had a certain glamour for me as it has for every Southerner, and I could see no reason why a fraternal order commemorating the deeds of the original Klansmen should not fill a need in the country today. I knew absolutely nothing about the structure of the new Ku Klux Klan, took it on faith, and assumed that in its government and administration, it would function like any other of the standard fraternal orders. I thought, from the meager information with which I was furnished, that I was thoroughly in accord with its principles, and that it would be more or less a pleasure to belong to it.

In the case of the Ku Klux Klan I took an immediate interest in the work of the organizer, brought him into touch with prominent friends of mine whom I induced to join, and did all I could to make his work a success. Shortly afterward I was made one of the organizers, and in this capacity devoted nearly all my time for three months to the work, conferring degrees, talking to people who were in favor of the Klan and to some who were opposed, and carefully studying the entire system of organization.

The fraternal order man who can really visualize an organization is the man who absorbs its work by observation and study, and there is no better method of doing this than performing the duties of an organizer. In my work as an organizer for the Knights of the Ku Klux Klan, I was first impressed with the fact, that, on account of its radical nature, it was dangerous. The first thing to which a candidate is enjoined is absolute secrecy. This is carried to the utmost extremity. A newly made "citizen" must not tell his wife or his family that he belongs to the organization, and must give no hint of it to his most intimate friends and business associates. I at once saw that any movement built along such a line was dangerous, regardless of its intentions, because secrecy of this sort places upon the organization the vital necessity of receiving as members only men of the highest character whose positions and reputations in the community would be an absolute safeguard against mischief. A secret organization composed of men of a low standard of civic responsibility would be the worst thing that could get into any community.

My experience as a fraternal order man has been that the personnel of the order varies with different localities. Therefore, while it might be perfectly proper to build a strictly secret organization in Kingsport, Tennessee, there might be, in another town an entirely different class of membership which would cause the movement to jeopardize the peace and dignity of the community. The potential danger of the Ku Klux organization in this respect was the first thing that dawned upon my consciousness, and it made me careful of the class of people whom I permitted to become members.

My duties took me into several towns, and night after night I administered the obligation and put on the degree work until I became thoroughly familiar with the mechanical end of it. Gradually, however, a feeling developed

within me that there was something wrong
with the organization — that it was not the
sort of "fraternal society" to which I had been
accustomed for nearly twenty years. I thought
at first that this was due to the fact tht I had
done so much lodge work in my lifetime that
I was growing stale. But certain portions of
the obligation, which at first had seemed merely
perfunctory, stood out in my mind and challenged serious thought and consideration.

I studied everything I could find to help me
in my work; I received printed matter from the
organization: I talked with Klansmen from
other cities; and I delved deeply into the origin
and history of the original Ku Klux Klan. But
business men of standing and prominence in
the places where I worked asked me pointed
questions about the organization, questions that
I could not answer and on which I could get no
satisfactory answers from above. Slowly my
vague fears that there was something vitally
wrong crystallized into stronger belief. I spoke
to a few close friends in the organization, and
asked them to give me their frank opinions
about it. Without any prompting from me
they voiced the same thoughts and gave expres-
sions to the same doubts I had myself.

After much thoughtful deliberation, I reached
the decision that the Ku Klux obligation was
radically wrong. It was not the kind of obligation men take in *fraternal* organizations — it
was a *political* obligation. I saw that the ritual,

which had previously been to me merely a
badly written mass of words was really a
sacriligious mockery. I realized that the whole
scheme was vicious in principle, and a menace
to the peace and safety of America. The basis
for these conclusions can be stated briefly:

First: While the organization was incorporated under the laws of the State of Georgia,
as a fraternal order, the claim being advanced
by the promoters that it should have similiar
powers to the Masons and Knights of Pythias,
it is not a fraternal organization in the sense
usually understood, but an attempt to create
in this republic of ours an "Invisible Empire,"
entirely political and military in nature and
designed to function bodily.

Second: The "Invisible Empire" is under the
control of one man who openly calls himself
an "Emperor," holds position for life, and exer-
cises despotic control over the affairs of the
organization.

Third: Candidates — designated as "aliens"
— who are received into the organization, are
not regarded as "members," but as "citizens"
of this "Invisible Empire," and instead of being
"initiated," as is usually the case in fraternal
orders, are "naturalized" and become "subjects" of the "Emperor."

Fourth: Membership is restricted to a limited
class of American citizens, including only white,
Gentile, American-born Protestants, all other
Americans being ineligible.

Fifth: In propagating this "Invisible Empire," the work, which is being done all over the United States by a highly paid and highly efficient field force, is being carried on by stirring up prejudice and hatred against the Catholic, the Jew, the negro, and the foreign-born American citizen.

Sixth: Under the claim of the enforcement of "law and order," the "Invisible Empire" is attempting to take into its grasp the entire law-enforcing machinery of the United States, including the officers and men of the Regular Army and Reserve Corps, the National Guard, sheriffs and their deputies, mayors, police officials and men, judges and all persons connected with law administration, with the exception of those ineligible under the rules above stated.

Seventh: The "citizens" of the "Invisible Empire" are urged by the organization to purchase white robes and helmets, which are used for the purpose of going abroad in disguise for the concealment of the identity of the wearer, and in many localities there have been parades and demonstrations of strength made by the organization, all having the effect of intimidating certain classes of people of these communities.

Eighth: The sale of these robes is a monopoly in the hands of the Gate City Manufacturing Company, a concern associated with the organization, and from this monopoly somebody is deriving an enormous revenue.

Ninth: The propagation of the organization is being conducted in such a way that it is clearly a money-making scheme run for the benefit of a few insiders.

Tenth: The claim that this is the "genuine original Klan" is a historical fraud, not supported by the history and prescript of the old Klan which are available for public inspection.

Eleventh: The Ku Klux propaganda is vicious, un-American and evil and will have a tendency to stir up racial and religious hatred in this country to such an extent as to result, unless checked, in a serious religious-racial war.

Twelfth: The ritualistic work, while clumsy, ignorant, plagiaristic, and poorly written is an attempt to use the cloak of religion to promote the financial fortunes of the insiders; and its principal feature — the ceremony of "naturalization"— is a mockery and parody on the sacred and holy rite of baptism.

Thirteenth: The organization should be exposed for what it is, and the Congress of the United States should enact suitable legislation to make it illegal and bar its literature and propaganda from the mails.

Fourteenth: Suitable and necessary legislation should be enacted by Congress and the State legislatures of a general nature which will forever prevent the organization and operation of a secret movement of this character.

The portentous nature of my conclusions, however, weighed heavily upon me, and after the most serious consideration, I finally decided to repudiate the entire organization, and as an American citizen to expose the whole system, calling public attention to what seems to me to be the greatest menace that has ever been launched in this country.

My decision to take this step was a most difficult one to reach. In the first place, to give to the public the facts and inside workings of the "Invisible Empire" means to subject oneself to the penalty of death for disclosing a secret of the order. This is stated unequivocally in the secret Ku Klux ritual. It also means becoming the target for a torrent of abuse that is likely to tear one to shreds before it has spent its fury.

The most disagreeable feature of the whole procedure is the absolute necessity of going on record publicly as violating a solemn oath, a pledge of honor, and an obligation that would ordinarily be considered sacred. Is a man, having taken an oath, ever justified in breaking it? In my opinion, when one is convinced that the oath in question is illegal, and that a certain portion of it is of a nature to incite riot and lawlessness, a man is not only justified in breaking it, but is morally required to break it. It is a public duty he owes the state. The inherent strength of the "Invisible Empire" lies in the fact that its "citizens" having once taken its vicious obligation will not dare to violate it.

I have, therefore, deliberately and with careful thought, decided to violate and repudiate this obligation, with the exception of a certain portion pledging allegiance to the Constitution of the United States and my State, which portion is, in my judgment, mere camouflage for the purpose of concealing the fangs of the rattlesnake. The question as to whether I am right or wrong is one that will have to be decided by public opinion. If I have divulged facts and exposed the secret workings of what is merely a *fraternal* organization, then I am unquestionably guilty of reprehensible conduct. If I am wrong in my viewpoint, I do not deserve to be allowed to mingle with honorable men and women, and should be set apart from my fellows as a social outcast.

On the other hand, if I am right in the stand that I take, that the Ku Klux Klan is a secret, political, military machine, actually developing into an "Invisible Empire" and possessing potentialities that may undermine the very idea of representative government; if I am correct in my position that the whole scheme is an attempt to create class hatred and antagonism, which in the end will array race against race, class against class, and religion against religion; if my contention is just that the proposition is a money-making scheme; and, if the public adopts my viewpoint to the extent of demanding that the organization be legislated out of existence and made an outlaw in the world of open things, then I shall feel satisfied that the violation of this oath has been a public service.

There is no middle ground. I am either entirely right, or else I am entirely wrong.

CHAPTER II

JOINING THE KU KLUX KLAN

MY first intimate contact with the "Invisible Empire" took place in upper East Tennessee, a section of the United States where one would least expect such a movement to take a definite foothold. There is practically no racial friction whatever in this section. The negro population is not large, and the negroes themselves are orderly and well-behaved people, industrious and well liked by the white people. A remarkable thing about East Tennessee is the scarcity of Jews. It is very doubtful if a careful search of the entire fifteen counties would disclose enough Jewish people to fill a synagogue. There is likewise a paucity of foreign population, for, with the exception of a few Greeks, the foreign element seems strangely absent. It is also remarkable that in this section the Roman Catholic religion does not seem to have been able to take root. While there is a small Catholic Church in Johnson City, and one in Greeneville that is opened but once a year, the other places have few, if any, Catholics in them. It is doubtful if one could find in all America a group of people who appear to be more overwhelmingly

Americans or more uniformly Protestant in their religious views than the inhabitants of this section.

In January, 1921, I was sent by a Chattanooga business house with which I had been connected for some time, on an extended trip through East Tennessee.

In February I arrived at Johnson City, intending to make that my headquarters and visit the other towns, which are easy of access. Early in March, 1921, I noticed a young man of pleasing personality, but I had never talked with him until the morning of March 16, when we were thrown together at the breakfast table.

"What are you selling?" I asked, taking it for granted that he was a traveling salesman.

He looked at the Masonic emblem I wore on my coat, smiled and handed me a clipping from the *Johnson City Staff*, stating that the organizer of the Ku Klux Klan was in town seeking recruits, but that people did not want the Klan, and expressing the hope that the vagrancy laws would take care of the worker for the movement.

My curiosity was immediately aroused, and after the organizer had carefully examined my Masonic and Knights of Pythias cards, we had a long talk together. He was an excellent salesman of his proposition, and in a few minutes he had me completely sold. In response to questions, I seemed to qualify, for the organizer, or Kleagle, as he is officially called, told me to hold myself in readiness and he would take me in that night. When evening came, I accompanied the Kleagle to the office of a prominent business man who had assembled his brother and his entire office force, and nine of us were taken into the "Invisible Empire," Knights of the Ku Klux Klan. The ceremony of "naturalization" was held in an inner office, the Kleagle wearing his white robe, with cape lined with red satin, and his peaked helmet with mask in which were cut two eye holes. It was my first glimpse of the Ku Klux regalia.

Next day, the Kleagle met me at breakfast again, and stated that he was compelled to go back to Knoxville, which was his headquarters, and asked me if I would not take hold of the work for a week, acting as his representative during his absence. He stated that, on account of newspaper opposition, he had been unable to make any rapid progress, but believed that on account of my more extensive acquaintance I could render some valuable service to the cause. This I agreed to do for him, and during the day was instructed in many matters connected with the soliciting work. On one point, he was very emphatic. "In your work," he said, "it is advisable to get the mayor, the sheriff and his deputies if they are eligible, and the police department. Also we want the telephone and telegraph people, and the better class of railroaders." With this special injunction, the Kleagle boarded the train for Knoxville, and left me in charge of the field, first notifying the Klansmen that he had so designated me.

On April 6, 1921, the Kleagle was suddenly called to Atlanta for a conference with the Imperial Kleagle, or chief organizer, and notified me that I should have to take charge of the work temporarily during his absence. He returned, however, on the evening of April 8, 1921, in time to obligate a class of thirty-six men whom I had waiting for him. He brought with him a commission as Kleagle made out in my name, and placed me in charge of the field, with the statement that he had been made a King Kleagle in another field. That night we conferred until very late, going over the entire work, and I had several papers which had to be made out. One of these papers was one of the most remarkable documents I have ever seen. It is called the "Kleagle's Pledge of Loyalty," and reads as follows:

"I, the undersigned, in order to be a regular appointed Kleagle of the Invisible Empire, Knights of the Ku Klux Klan (Incorporated), do freely and voluntarily promise, pledge and fully guarantee a lofty respect, whole-hearted loyalty and unwavering devotion at all times and under all circumstances and conditions from this day and date forward to William Joseph Simmons as Imperial Wizard and Emperor of the Invisible Empire, Knights of the Ku Klux Klan (Incorporated). I shall work in all respects in perfect harmony with him and under his authority and directions, in all his plans for the extension and government of the Society, and under his directions, with any and all of my officially superior officers duly appointed by him.

"I shall at any and all times be faithful and true in all things, and most especially in preventing and suppressing any factions, cisms or conspiracies against him or his plans and purposes for the peace and harmony of the Society which may arise or attempt to rise. I shall discourage and strenuously oppose any degree of disloyalty or disrespect on the part of myself or any klansman, anywhere and at any time or place, towards him as the founder and as the supreme chief governing head of the Society above named.

"This pledge, promise and guarantee I make as a condition precedent to my appointment stated above, and the continuity of my appointment as a Kleagle, and it is fully agreed that any deviation by me from this pledge will instantly automatically cancel and completely void my appointment together with all its prerogatives, my membership in the Society, and I shall forfeit all remunerations which may be then due me.

"I make this solemn pledge on my Oath of Allegiance and on my integrity and honor as a man and as a klansman, with serious purpose to keep same inviolate."

It will be noted in studying the foregoing document that the pledge is not to the organization, but to *William Joseph Simmons*.

In addition to this "pledge of loyalty" to "Emperor" Simmons, I was also required to sign an application for an indemnity bond, which was an agreement, not to indemnify the organization from loss, but to indemnify *William J. Simmons* in the sum of one thousand dollars. The application for employment, which in my case, was made after I was employed, was also directed to the "Emperor."

CHAPTER III

MY WITHDRAWAL

IT is doubtful if one could find anywhere in the country a finer, cleaner or better lot of men than those among whom I worked as an agent of Ku Kluxism. As individuals they were successful business and professional men, nearly all of them devout church members, married men with families, and just the sort of men to make up a prosperous community; yet, in spite of all this it seemed to me that the protection afforded by membership in an ultra secret movement like the "Invisible Empire" tended to inculcate lawlessness even among some of them. There is but little original law-breaking in this world. Most of it is due to precedent or suggestion. The power of suggestion is one of the most potent factors in every phase of human activity, and I believe that the mere fact of being a member of an organization that can go abroad in the land white-robed and masked is a suggestive force that encourages men to take the law into their own hands.

Two striking illustrations of this point recall themselves to my mind. In one case a man who stood very high in the Johnson City Klan was talking with me about a public demonstration.

He stated that he was not in favor of making any show of strength until the Klan had at least five hundred members, then he wanted to have everybody put on their robes, pile into automobiles and parade the streets. I called his attention to the provisions of the Code of Tennessee in reference to wearing masks in public.

"Oh, that's all right," he replied, "when we are fully organized the Klan will control the politics of this town. We will apply for a permit, and if we don't get it, we will parade anyhow. Nobody will dare stop us."

The other instance was a conversation I had with a man with whom I was most friendly. He was a younger man than the one just mentioned, but is considered a person of responsibility and good judgment. It happened that the largest restaurant in Johnson City is owned and operated by Greeks, and this man seemed to be especially hostile to foreigners. In discussing them one day he said to me:

"I don't like to see these Greeks make such progress here. They are driving good Americans out of business. We've got twenty-eight robes in our lodge room, and I am in favor of getting a bunch some night, breaking open their restaurant and dumping all their fixtures and merchandise into the streets. That will serve as an object lesson that they are not wanted in Johnson City."

Now, from my knowledge of that man, I do not believe that he would deliberately violate

the law. In fact, if I were sheriff of his county
and wanted a real man to head a posse, I would
call on this man and swear him in as a deputy.
I doubt very much if he would even lead a mob
of masked men to tear up a Greek restaurant,
but the mob spirit was there, and it was put
there because he was a member of the Ku
Klux Klan.

The old Ku Klux Klan performed its functions, not so much by overt acts, as by creating
the impression of what it could do and by
inspiring terror in the minds of the people it
desired to reach. It operated largely on the
principle of suggestion. It soon began to appear
to me that the modern movement began to
plant evil suggestions in the minds of some of
its members, almost from the time they became
connected with the organization.

From the very first time that a Ku Klux
organizer set foot in town, the *Johnson City Staff*
had fearlessly and vigorously condemned the
movement and advised its readers to have
nothing to do with it. As the movement began
to grow, many of the leading business men
became Klansmen. They were nearly all advertisers in the local paper. The attacks on the
Klan by the *Staff* were the subjects of many
discussions, and it was decided to "put a
muzzle on the paper." Accordingly many
advertisers quietly suggested to the publisher
of the paper that he "lay off" the Ku Klux
Klan. Whether this advice was accompanied

by threats or by the actual withdrawal of business, I do not know, but I do know that the *Staff* suddenly "pulled in its horns" and remained muzzled up to the time I left the territory. This incident is cited to show the power of this ultra-secret system in effectively paralyzing the freedom of the press, and what has doubtless happened in other towns and cities where Ku Kluxism has thoroughly inoculated communities with its deadly poison.

While working among the different towns in my territory, we noticed in the papers occasionally a reference to some act of lawlessness or violence committed in other States by men disguised in white robes and masks. As the details, at the time, were very meager, and as the Atlanta headquarters denied that any of the members of the Ku Klux Klan were connected with them, the Klansmen in my field paid but little attention to these outrages. In fact, I, myself, did not believe that the organization could be guilty of committing such open and flagrant outrages, until I had a conversation with the King Kleagle some time around June 1, 1921. I had met him at Knoxville for the purpose of urging that the charters for three towns be immediately granted. He began talking about the work of the other Klans, and stated that in Houston, Texas, a young negro, charged with familiarity with white women, had been taken out into the country and mutilated. The King Kleagle said that this was

done by the Houston Klan, which ran things
its own way, as it had the mayor, the police
force and practically all of the politicians.

During the months of May and the early
part of June, 1921, while following a busy
routine, I began studying the Ku Klux movement and going carefully into every detail that
suggested itself. I had already become suspi-
cious of the movement as a result of the apparent
"one man power" of Simmons as exemplified in
his scheme of employment of Kleagles; the
questions that had been asked me had started a
second line of investigation; and then a third
cause of dissatisfaction arose from a feeling of
disgust at the way in which the work was
propagated. I jumped at no hasty conclusions
in the matter, but a gradual feeling of revolt
against the movement developed in my mind,
which feeling I communicated to a few friends.
I also asked several members of the organization, with whom I was intimately acquainted,
what they thought of the organization, and I
found that my own doubts and fears were
shared by them. The leader of the Kingsport
Klan was an out-and-out skeptic on the whole
movement. Then again, from inquiries I had
made as to the work in near-by towns outside
my territory, I learned that Kleagles were
selling memberships as they would sell insurance
or stock.

Although I was supposed to canvass for members, I made it a rule, during my period of

service as Kleagle, to do no soliciting whatever. My system was to establish a membership committee in each community in my territory and permit the committees to select their own material. This policy made the personnel in my territory very high, as each individual was elected to membership before he was invited to join the organization.

In addition to its field force, the propagation department of the Ku Klux Klan, I learned, uses motion pictures and paid lecturers to spread the germs of Ku Kluxism. There is a picture entitled, "The Face at Your Window" that is being used extensively as an aid to the canvassing Kleagles. The film company arranges with the local Kleagle to have this picture exhibited on a certain day, and each Klansman is requested to bring a friend with him to see it. At the close of the performance the Klansman hands his friend an application blank and through the psychological effect of the picture usually gets the other to join. The system of using lecturers seems to help considerably to swell the Ku Klux roster.

Still another method of winning members was by newspaper advertising. The Exalted Cyclops, the head, of the Knoxville Klan showed me the copy for a full page advertisement that his Klan intended inserting in the Knoxville papers to secure the five hundred membership necessary before their Klan could procure a charter. I saw that such wholesale solicitation of members could have but one result — inevitably the control of this secret organization would pass into hands least competent to exercise it.

As I became more familiar with the movement, as it was being propagated elsewhere, and from my own study and observation, I reached some definite conclusions. From the first, I had observed carefully the classes of men who were being enrolled, the motives for their enlisting, and the effect the organization had upon them. The result as a whole had been disturbing, but it was from my study of the organization itself that I finally turned in revulsion from it. It was not easy to get the real facts. I asked many questions, both in writing and orally, of the King Kleagle, some of which he could answer, but most of them he could not. The Constitution of the organization I could not get. The King Kleagle had no copy and had never seen a copy. It was not until a short time before my withdrawal that I was shown the constitution and the reading of the document confirmed all too well the suspicions I had already formed about the menace that lay in Ku Kluxism. That it was a political money-making scheme rather than a fraternal order, I began to comprehend from the sales-methods I saw around me. It also seemed to me that there were certain potential dangers inherent in it. When I had once asked the King Kleagle how a Klan should function when once it was organized, "Tell them," he had answered, "to clean up their towns." That "cleaning up a town" by illegal means could end only in mob rule was clear enough to any thinking man, and the fact that the newspapers had been reporting outrages in various Southern States — outrages committed by masked men — did not make me feel any more comfortable.

Oppressed therefore by its potential dangers, disgusted with a ritualistic work which really seemed to me a sacrilege, and revolted by the spirit of religious and racial hatred which it inculcated, I decided to resign my work as Kleagle, and accordingly mailed my resignation to the King Kleagle on June 15, 1921.

My resignation as Kleagle was reluctantly accepted by J. M. McArthur, the King Kleagle, who wrote me to that effect and asked me to meet him in Chattanooga for the purpose of securing my final release, which was given me the latter part of June, 1921. While my name was never mentioned, the exposure of the Klan which was made by the *World* brought forth the statement from the Atlanta headquarters that "the individual responsible for the attack had been discharged from the propagation department for conduct and character unbecoming a gentleman." As a matter of fact, I have in my possession a letter from McArthur expressing "genuine regret" at my resignation, warmly commending me for "excellent work," and granting me "an honorable discharge from the

propagation department of the Knights of the
Ku Klux Klan." Fortunately for the cause of
decent Americanism, King Kleagle McArthur
is one of these "ready letter-writers," and the
letters written by him to me have all been filed
away. Some of them were valuable pieces of
documentary evidence to sustain the case made
against the Klan by the *World*.

I was invited by McArthur to attend two
meetings of the Klan in Chattanooga, where I
found the movement strongly organized. At
one of these meetings the leader of the local
Klan, a physician, made one of the most incendiary speeches I have ever heard, a speech that
was vociferously applauded by a large gathering
of Klansmen. He made a violent attack on
Jews, Negroes and Catholics, and stated that:
"the Knights of Columbus have 2,000 rifles
stored in the Catholic church; they will before
long march down Market Street armed with
their rifles; and the Ku Klux Klan must
organize and arm itself for the purpose of
protecting the city from the designs of this
murderous organization."

Having resigned from the propagation department, I then withdrew from "citizenship" in
the "Invisible Empire," and denounced it
in the *World* and its associated newspapers.
Although my letter was registered and mailed
to *William J. Simmons* personally, I never
received any reply. The letter read as follows:

"You are hereby notified that I have this day voluntarily withdrawn as a 'citizen' of the 'Invisible Empire,' Knights of the Ku Klux Klan, Inc., and shall no longer consider myself in any way connected with the organization. After five months of 'citizenship' in the 'Invisible Empire,' three months of which were spent as a Kleagle, I have reached the conclusion that your proposition is a historical fraud; that it is a money-making scheme run for the benefit of a few insiders; that it is engaged in an evil propaganda in promoting unwarranted religious and racial hatred against Jews, Roman Catholics, negroes, and foreign-born American citizens; that your entire scheme is a dangerous public menace that will inevitably lead to bloodshed and if successful must result in revolution; and that, in the interests of decent Americanism, it should be suppressed by the Federal and State authorities.

"I further notify you that I utterly repudiate and refuse to be bound in any way by any and all portions of the 'oath of allegiance' to the 'Invisible Empire' formerly taken by me, excepting that portion pledging allegiance to the Constitution of the United States and of my State, with which portion you have camouflaged the real purport and meaning of the oath. The remainder of the oath conflicts with a higher obligation I have previously assumed as an officer of the Reserve Corps of the United States Army. I therefore denounce said remaining portions of said oath as illegal, and detrimental to the fundamental principles which underlie the entire legal structure of this country. I further decline, any longer, to keep secret any part or parts of your scheme to establish in free America an 'Invisible Empire' fraudulent in its conception, vicious in its nature, political in its objects, and subject to the will of a self-constituted 'Emperor' who seeks to exploit the American people for his own personal aggrandizement.

"In defiance of your threats of 'dishonor, disgrace, and death' as contained in your ritual — written and copyrighted by yourself — I denounce your ritualistic work as an insult to all Christian people in America, as an attempt to hypocritically obtain money from the public under the cloak of sanctimonious piety; and, I charge that the principal feature of your ceremony of 'naturalization' into the 'Invisible Empire' is a blasphemous and sacrilegious mockery of the holy rite of baptism, wherein for political and financial purposes, you have polluted with your infamous parody those things that Christians, regardless of creed or dogma, hold most sacred.

"I further charge that when in your printed literature you claim that your organization is the 'genuine original Klan,' this statement is a fraud historically and a fraud in principle. While you have — without any right whatever — appropriated to yourself the name, regalia, and certain nomenclature of the original Klan, your scheme is radically different in conception, in organization, and in purpose. A careful study, which I have made, of the Prescript of the original Klan and all available history and literature on the subject, reveals the fact that there is little, if anything, in common between the two organizations. Your false pretenses of 'genuineness' are therefore insults to the history, the traditions, and the entire record of the South.

"Ever since your scheme has been actively propagated, there has been a wave of crime in the Southern States, consisting to a large extent of 'private regulations' of the public peace, committed by men who have gone about their respective communities wearing disguises and taking into their own hands the functions of prosecuting attorney, witnesses, judge, jury and executioner, in direct contravention to the Bill of Rights of the Federal and State constitutions. Men have been dragged from their beds at night, forcibly abducted on the streets and in their homes, arrested without warrant on the public streets, conveyed to secluded places, there to be flogged, tarred and feathered. In two instances helpless women, after being stripped of their clothing, have been similarly maltreated. In nearly every reported case, the perpetrators of these acts of lawlessness have worn disguises, described as 'masks and white robes,' which description

correspond convincingly with the official regalia of the
'Invisible Empire.' In three specific cases, acts of lawlessness have been so openly and flagrantly committed
by members of the 'Ku Klux Klan,' that you have been
compelled to take official cognizance. In these three
instances where responsibility has been fixed, it was very
evident that the illegal oath and the secret teachings of
your 'Invisible Empire' were construed by your dupes
as granting a license to engage in secret regulation of the
peace by means of anonymous warnings, threats, intimi-
dations, abduction, the whip, and the use of tar and
feathers. Having studied your scheme, both from the
inside and the outside, I have no doubt whatever that
practically all of these reported outrages were committed
by members of your organization. If it were proven,
however, that your 'citizens' were not *prima facie* responsible, at the same time there exists a moral responsibility,
because when one group of people is permitted to go about
in disguise, it places the community at the mercy of any
group which cares to adopt similar tactics.

"Everywhere the promoters of your scheme have gone,
they have sought to enlist as 'citizens' the white, Gentile,
Protestant public officials, especially those having in
charge the enforcement of the law. No matter how capable, how efficient, and how conscientious a public official
may be, if he chances to be a Jew or a Catholic, you not
only do not want him, but your organization is now
planning actively to cause all the Jews, Catholics, and
foreign-born naturalized Americans in this country to be
removed from public life. Aside from vicious politics,
and in view of the fact that your oath is an accessory
before the fact to mob violence, this tampering and
meddling with the law-enforcing machinery of the country
— under the alleged plea of 'law and order'— is a direct
blow at the entire legal machinery of the United States,
a condition that, in its nature, approaches anarchy.

"At a time when peaceful relations are existing between
the white and black races, you are disrupting the industrial
conditions of the South, by your anti-negro propaganda

and causing a state of unrest that can result only in dangerous and mischievous consequences. In your anti-Catholic and anti-Jewish propaganda, your organization is scattering broadcast over this country wicked, malicious and inflammatory lies about American citizens of those religious beliefs, lies that brand your movement as being far more vicious than the insidious German propaganda in this country prior to our entrance into the recent war. You are publishing, for example, the statement that the Jews are seeking to promote a race war between white people and negroes, and the intimation that the Catholic Church was responsible for the murder of President Abraham Lincoln. In public statements, you and your paid speakers give expression to wordy, sanctimonious and high-sounding platitudes, while secretly your propagandists, in a sneaking and contemptible manner, are spreading poisonous and vicious lies they dare not give voice to in public.

"Your 'Invisible Empire' is furthermore a money-making scheme! You, yourself, an individual of little, if any, means prior to your becoming an 'Emperor' have so far received from 'friends' a $25,000 residence completely furnished! Your connection with the organization is either bringing you large sums of money at present, or the promise of the same in the future! You are allowed to appropriate to your own use all of the ten dollars "donated" by any person whose application you personally solicit! All of the rituals and other printed publications of your organization are copyrighted in your name, and it is presumable that you have either received royalties for their use or a cash consideration for their sale! Your organization has recently bought Lanier University, of which you have been made the head, and college presidents are usually paid salaries! While orders for robes at $6.50 are taken in your name, they are filled by the Gate City Manufacturing Company, at a substantial profit, and the public has not been informed as to the disposition of this huge amount of funds! The Searchlight Publishing Company, headed by your Imperial

Kleagle is no doubt a big revenue producer! Your Imperial Kleagle is also the head of the Clarke Realty Company, in whose operations, I have no doubt you are also interested! These varied financial operations indicate to me that spreading religious and racial hatred is a lucrative business for you and your associates.

"Your whole 'Invisible Empire' is a cancer in the body politic! It is like some foul and loathsome thing that grows and flourishes in the dark, away from the sight of honest men and women. It was conceived in avarice, sired in ignorance, and dammed in greed. It is now being nurtured in cunning and false pretense, and fed upon an unholy lust for gold, by means of passion, hatred, and the prejudice of religious and racial fanaticism. And, day by day, with your oily assurance, you say that these devilish devices of discord are being developed in the name of 'pure Americanism' ! If this is your idea of America, you haven't the slightest conception of what pure Americanism means!

"There is no place in America for an 'Invisible Empire' of hate and venom; and there is no provision in the laws of this country for an 'Emperor' ! The 'Invisible Empire' should be made visible! It should be held up to the light so that honest men can see its ugly structure and analyze its nefarious potentialities, and then, having seen this monstrosity, the people should demand of their legally constituted forces of government that Ku Kluxism and the Ku Klux Klan be outlawed and barred forever from operating in this free Republic.

Yours truly,

HENRY P. FRY."

CHAPTER IV

WHAT IS THE "INVISIBLE EMPIRE?"

A STUDY of the physical structure of the "Invisible Empire" necessarily starts with its corporate organization, its officers, its general method of functioning, and its ramifications throughout the United States. Although organized under the pretense that it is a "fraternal order," a close investigation of the system reveals the fact that its activities extend in several directions. Its three principal promoters, William J. Simmons, Edward Young Clarke and Mrs. M. E. Tyler, are engaged in several lines of business all of which are closely related. The show under the main tent is the "Invisible Empire," Knights of the Ku Klux Klan, Inc., allied to which either directly or indirectly is the "Gate City Manufacturing Company," a corporation organized under the laws of the State of Georgia for the manufacture of lodge regalia, etc., the Searchlight Publishing Company, which prints a weekly paper which is recognized by the public as the official organ of Ku Kluxism, and Lanier University, which was acquired in August, 1921, and of which William J. Simmons is the president. There is also the Clarke Realty Company in which E. Y. Clarke and Mrs.

M. E. Tyler are mentioned as incorporators, the operations of which corporation are not known.

The charter of the Knights of the Ku Klux Klan granted by the Superior Court of Fulton County, Georgia, reads as follows:

"GEORGIA, FULTON COUNTY.

TO THE SUPERIOR COURT OF SAID COUNTY:

The petition of W. J. SIMMONS, H. D. SHACKLEFORD, E. R. CLARKSON, J. B. FROST, W. L. SMITH, R. C. W. RAMSPECK, G. D. COUCH, L. M. JOHNSON, A. G. DALLAS, W. E. FLODING, W. C. BENNETT, J. F. V. SAUL, all of said State and County, respectfully shows:

1. That they desire for themselves, their associates and successors to be incorporated in the State of Georgia for the period of twenty years, with the right of renewal; when and as provided by law, as a *patriotic, secret, social, benevolent order* under the name and style of

'KNIGHTS OF THE KU KLUX KLAN'

2. The purpose and object of said corporation is to be purely benevolent and eleesmosynary, and there shall be no capital stock or profit or gain to the members thereof.

3. The principal office and place of business shall be in Fulton County, Georgia, but petitioners desire that the corporation shall have the power to issue decrees, edicts and certificates of organization to subordinate branches of the corporation in this or other States of the United States and elsewhere, whenever the same shall be deemed desirable in the conduct of its business.

4. The petitioners desire that the Society shall have the power to confer an initiative degree ritualism, fraternal and secret obligations, words, grip signs and ceremonies under which there shall be united only white male persons of sound health, good morals and high character; and further desire such rights, powers and privileges as are now extended to the Independent Order of Odd Fellows, Free and Accepted Masons, Knights of Pythias, *et al.*,

under and by virtue of the laws of the State of Georgia.

5. Petitioners desire that there shall be a Supreme Legislative Body in which "shall be vested the power to adopt and amend constitutions and by-laws for the regulation of the general purpose and welfare of the order, and of the subordinate branches of same.

6. Petitioners desire that the 'IMPERIAL KLONVOKA-TION' (Supreme Legislative Body) shall be composed of the SUPREME OFFICERS AND 'KLOPPERS' (DELEGATES selected by the 'KLORO' (STATE CONVENTION) of the SEVERAL 'REALMS' (subordinate jurisdiction); and of such other persons as the constitution and by-laws of the Society may provide.

7. Petitioners desire that the business of the Society shall be under the control of the 'IMPERIAL WIZARD' (PRESIDENT), who shall be amenable in his official administration to the 'IMPERIAL KLONCILIUM' (Supreme Executive Committee), a majority of whom shall have authority to act, and a two-thirds' majority power to veto the official acts of the 'IMPERIAL WIZARD' (PRESIDENT) in the matters pertaining to the general welfare of the Society; and to contract with other members of the Society for the purpose of promoting and conducting its interests and general welfare, in any way, manner, or method he may deem proper for the Society's progress and stability, subject to the restrictions of the power of the 'IMPERIAL WIZARD' (PRESIDENT) as is heretofore set forth in this paragraph.

8. Petitioners desire that they shall have the right to adopt a constitution and by-laws and elect the first KLONCILIUM (Supreme Executive Committee), which shall possess all the powers of the 'IMPERIAL KLONVOKA-TION (Supreme Legislative Body) until the first organization and meeting of that body, and shall fix the number, title and terms of officers composing said 'KLONCILIUM' (Supreme Legislative Committee).

9. Petitioners desire the right to own separate unto itself and to control the sale of all paraphernalia, regalia, stationery, jewelry and such other materials needed by the subordinate branches of the order for the proper

conduct of their business; the right to publish a fraternal
magazine and such other literature as is needed in the
conduct of the business of the order; the right to buy,
hold and sell real estate and personal property suitable
to the purpose of the said corporation; to sell, exchange
or sublease the same or any part thereof; to mortgage or
create liens thereon; to borrow money and secure the payment thereof by mortgage or deed of trust and to appoint
trustees in connection therewith; to execute promissory
notes, to have and to use a common seal; to sue and be
sued; to plead and be impleaded; to do and perform all
these things and exercise all those rights, which under the
laws of Georgia, are conferred upon societies or orders of
like character.

10.   *Wherefore* petitioners pray an order incorporating
them, their associates and successors under the name and
style aforesaid with all the powers and privileges necessary to the extension of the order or the conduct of the
business and purposes of like nature."

The casual examination of the above instrument fails to show anything more significant
than the fact that it is a simple application for
a charter for an ordinary fraternal organization, several of whom, including the Masonic
fraternity and the Knights of Pythias, it
specifically names. An analysis, however, of
the instrument reveals some interesting things,
and raises some questions that may be of
service to the public in dealing with Ku Kluxism.

In the first place, this charter, which was
granted July 1, 1916, confers upon W. J.
Simmons and certain associates the right to
engage in the business of a fraternal society
under the name and style of "KNIGHTS OF THE
KU KLUX KLAN." As a matter of fact the

propagation of the movement goes forward under the name and title of "Invisible Empire, Knights of the Ku Klux Klan, Inc." The use of the words "Invisible Empire" in connection with the authorized and legal title of the organization is an *ultra vires* act without the sanction of the Georgia law under which the society is operating.

The following copy of the application for charter membership illustrates this point:

"To His MAJESTY, THE IMPERIAL WIZARD, EMPEROR OF THE INVISIBLE EMPIRE, KNIGHTS OF THE KU KLUX KLAN (INC.):

I, the undersigned, a native-born, true and loyal citizen of the United States of America, being a white Gentile person of temperate habits, sound in mind, and a believer in the tenets of the Christian religion, the maintenance of *white supremacy*, the practice of an honorable clanishness and the principles of "pure Americanism," do voluntarily most respectfully, seriously and unselfishly petition you for *citizenship* in the INVISIBLE EMPIRE, KNIGHTS OF THE KU KLUX KLAN, and be a *charter member* of a Klan located at.................State of.........

I guarantee on my honor to conform strictly to all rules and requirements regulating my "naturalization" and the continuance of my membership, and at all times a strict and loyal obedience to your constitutional authority and the constitution and laws, and all regulations and usages of the fraternity. The required "donation" accompanies this petition.

Signed: ...., *Petitioner*.

Date........................192....

Residence Address..

Business Address ....

Endorsers will sign on other side.

Notice: Check the address to which mail may be sent."

75M–4–15–21

This is the standard form for application for "citizenship" and several hundred such applications, properly signed, have come under my personal observation. It is distinctly a request to be "naturalized" as a "citizen" of the "Invisible Empire," Knights of the Ku Klux Klan, and not an application for membership in an order known as the "Knights of the Ku Klux Klan" by itself.

It appears from an examination of the records, that the Knights of the Ku Klux Klan made but little headway for several years, when it was under the sole management of William J. Simmons. An examination of the Atlanta City Directory reveals the fact that the present "Emperor" was engaged in other lines of activity, largely as a professional organizer. In 1915 he appears listed as "Organizer, of the Woodmen of the World"; in 1916, "Imperial Wizard and founder of the Knights of the Ku Klux Klan"; in 1918, the next year a directory was issued, as "State Manager, Heralds of Liberty"; in 1920, as "Lecturer"; and in 1921, again as "Imperial Wizard, Knights of the Ku Klux Klan." It was not, apparently, until he joined forces with Edward Young Clarke, that the enterprise was placed on a paying basis. Clarke, it is said, has had wide experience as a professional propagandist, and prior to his taking charge of the Ku Klux movement was employed to raise money for the Anti-Saloon League and the Salvation Army, conducting drives for those bodies. The city directory of Atlanta lists him as follows: 1915, "Secretary, Brooks County Industrial Club"; 1916, Secretary, "Georgia Chamber of Commerce"; 1918, "Secretary, Southeastern Exhibit Association; 1920–21, "President Southern Publicity Association." Under the direction of Clarke the entire system of field work has been perfected, and as Imperial Kleagle, Clarke is responsible for the success of the movement.

Clarke, whose chief helper and backer was Mrs. Elizabeth Tyler, was conducting the Southern Publicity Bureau at the time, and quickly saw the big financial possibilities which lay in the capitalization of the name "Ku Klux." Simmons, who had concocted the scheme of organization which placed the "entire works" into his own hands, lacked the ability to put his ideas into execution. At this point, I should like to take issue with practically every man who had made any attack on the Ku Klux Klan. The general opinion has been that "Simmons is absolutely sincere in what he is doing, but has been in the hands of Clarke and Mrs. Tyler." I have never met Simmons in person, but I have studied his organization in the most minute detail. From my study of the system and the part the man has played in it, I believe that he is a cunning, shrewd adventurer, who, from the start conceived the idea of acquiring both wealth and unlimited power from his secret "Invisible Empire." In all of his public utterances in the newspapers and before Congress he has shown a shiftiness and evasiveness clearly discernible amid a vast mass of wordiness.

In his entire scheme of organization and management, he has so constructed his proposition that he is master of the situation with practically unlimited power. In this particular a good illustration can be found in the contract he made with Clarke whereby the latter became the Chief Sales Manager of the membership peddlers for the whole country. This contract, while it gives Clarke the opportunity of making a vast sum of money, at the same time makes Simmons the absolute dictator of Clarke's movements. The probabilities are that Simmons, realizing that he himself was ignorant of real organization methods, so framed this contract that he could let Clarke out at any time, and take over to himself the functions of the propagation department after he had learned the system.

The contract which brought Clarke and Mrs. Tyler into the organization reads as follows:

"STATE OF GEORGIA, County of Fulton,

"This agreement, made and entered into on this the seventh day of June, A.D. 1920, by and between the Knights of the Ku Klux Klan, a corporation of said county, acting by its Imperial Wizard (President), W. J. Simmons, party of the first part, and Edward Young Clarke, of said county, party of the second part.

"Witnesseth, that the said party of the second part hereto having, by virtue of this agreement, been appointed Imperial Kleagle (General Superintendent of the organization department) of said first party, and it being desirable that the details of his rights, privileges, powers, duties, responsibilities, and compensation, etc., in addition to that laid down in the constitution and laws of the said corporation be definitely fixed:

"Therefore, it is agreed by the said parties hereto that this contract shall continue so long as it is mutually agreeable; that it shall remain of force and may be canceled by either party hereto without previous notice of any intention to do so.

"It is agreed that said second party may employ, subject to the approval and appointment of the said Imperial Wizard (President) of the corporation aforesaid, and subject to the right and power of said Imperial Wizard (President) to revoke all such appointments, such assistant organizers as he (the said second party) may deem necessary to properly carry out the plans for the propagation and extension of said corporation; provided, that such persons so appointed or employed be members of the said corporation in good and regular standing prior to their appointment, and that they maintain their good standing therein as an essential condition on which their appointment is made.

"It is agreed that in all things the second party shall be subordinate to the said Imperial Wizard (President), and shall attempt no plans or methods of work without the consent or approval of the said Imperial Wizard.

"It is agreed that the said second party shall receive as in full compensation and expenses of himself and his duly appointed and commissioned subordinate organizers the sum of $8.00 for each and every new member brought into the said corporation by himself and his assistant subordinate organizers, and in addition to the $8.00 he shall receive $2.00 for each new member added to all Klans organized by himself or his subordinate organizers within a period of six months after the date of the charter of all such Klans organized by himself and his subordinate organizers.

"It is agreed that no expense or debts shall be made or

incurred by the said Edward Young Clarke or his subordinate organizers, and no obligation entered into with
any firm, company, corporation, or person for which the
said first party hereto or the said Imperial Wizard
(President) shall be bound to make any outlay of or
expenditure of money, unless there be a specific approval
of the particular item or items of all such expenditures,
prior to the incurring of same by the said Imperial Wizard
(President) of the said corporation.

"It is agreed that the said second party shall advance,
from time to time, as may be necessary the office rent and
all other expenses incident to the proper conduct and
furnishing of the main office of the aforesaid corporation,
and in addition thereto a sum of not less than $75 per
week and traveling expenses of the said Imperial Wizard
(President) of the aforesaid corporation, reimbursing himself for such expenditures out of the $2.00 due by him to
the aforesaid corporation on account of each member
received into the aforesaid corporation by him and his
duly appointed and commissioned subordinate organizers.

"Duly executed in duplicate in the city of Atlanta, Ga.,
on the day and date above written.

"KNIGHTS OF THE KU KLUX KLAN, INC.
    "By W. J. SIMMONS, Imperial Wizard (President).
                "EDWARD YOUNG CLARKE."

As is well known the new Ku Klux Klan, like
the old, depends to a great extent upon concealing the identity of the members by the
means of long white robes and a white peaked
helmet, with hangings in which eye holes have
been cut. In the old Klan these robes were
made by members of the Klansmen's family,
but in the new order of affairs the work of
supplying these robes is a monopoly entirely in
the hands of the national organization.

Members are not actually required to possess a robe, but it is generally the case that every man who comes into the movement is childishly eager to acquire one, whether he can use it in public or not. The organization does not "sell" the robes to members; it merely rents them, and members upon leaving the organization are required to return them to the head of the local Klan. The price charged a member for a robe is $6.50, while the Kleagle must pay $12 as his robe has more trimming. Made in large quantities, as they are being made, there ought to be a profit of at least $5 per garment, although I believe a New York garment maker could show a larger profit than that. According to "Emperor" Simmons, the present output is about six hundred robes a day. Orders are taken for the garments by Kleagles and Exalted Cyclops of the different Klans on measuring blanks printed especially for the purpose. The order is made out and addressed to the "Imperial Wizard," but it is filled by the "Gate City Manufacturing Company" of Atlanta, Georgia. The records of Fulton County, Georgia, show that application for charter for this corporation was filed June 9, 1920, with C. B. Davis and Lottie B. Davis as incorporators. It shows a capital stock of $25,000, and states that "more than $5,000 has been paid in." It also asks the right to increase its capitalization to $50,000. Its powers indicate that it is to engage in the manufacture and sale of lodge supplies, paraphernalia and equipment of all sorts for the use of lodges, secret societies, etc. The corporation apparently lay dormant for a year, as an order of court allowing the petition was only allowed on August 19, 1921. Until the incorporators met and organized there could have been no legal organization of the corporation. No reports as to business done had been filed in Fulton County up to the date of the court order above mentioned. This concern, however, has been doing business for several months prior to that time, as I received several shipments from them in April and May 1921. *Who owns the Gate City Manufacturing Company? What connection has it with the Knights of the Ku Klux Klan? What becomes of the enormous profit derived from the sales of robes?*

During the summer of 1921, the Knights of the Ku Klux Klan purchased the handsome, colonial home of H. M. Durant on Peachtree Road, about five miles from Atlanta, at an approximate cost of $75,000. The purchase comprises a block of land about four hundred feet square. Extensive improvements, worthy of a real emperor's palace are contemplated for this property, and it will be the headquarters of the "Imperial Palace." The land will be cut up into gardens, small lakes and building sites. It is estimated that $30,000 worth of marble alone will be used. A handsome statue of General N. B. Forrest will be erected, and also a statue of "Emperor" William J. Simmons.

There will be electric fountains, electric fiery crosses, lakes, boat houses and tennis courts. According to the "Emperor": "There will be no manufacturing handled at the Palace. We now have a paraphernalia plant here turning out six hundred robes a day, in addition to other equipment, and we expect to erect in a short time a building with railroad frontage to be devoted exclusively to manufacturing." It is also planned to take over a large printing plant. If this extensive program is carried out, there will be a huge enterprise with all the combined activities costing not less than $3,500,000.

While the organization has been buying land and engaging in real estate transactions, the Imperial Kleagle, as a side line, has also gone into the real estate business. On June 27, 1921, a petition was filed for charter for the "Clarke Realty Company" with Edward Young Clarke and Mrs. Elizabeth Tyler as incorporators, with authorized capital stock of $10,000 with privilege of increasing it to $100,000. The corporation seeks the right to deal generally in real estate. Just what real estate the "Clarke Realty Company" has bought, sold, leased, rented, or exchanged or acted as brokers for, has not appeared in print.

The functions of Clarke appear to be exclusively to propagate the work and organize Klans, after which they are turned over to Simmons. According to a statement made by Clarke to the *World* the organization has one

thousand chartered Klans, it requiring the
services of two people engaged every day to
write charters. After the Klans are chartered
they are turned over to Simmons. In this
connection, it would be well to turn back to
the charter and note that under Section 7, the
"business of the society shall be under the
control of the IMPERIAL WIZARD (PRESIDENT),"
etc. This control is so thorough that in the secret
constitution of the organization the term of
office of the president is for life, and he can be
removed only by the unanimous vote of his
Imperial Kloncilium. The constitution also
provides as follows:

"Article I, Section 2. The government of this order
shall ever be military in character, most especially its
management and control; and no legislative enactment or
constitutional amendment hereafter forever shall encroach
upon, effect or change this essential, fundamental principle
of this order — The Invisible Empire.

"Section 2. The government of this order shall be
invested primarily in the Imperial Wizard, as Commander-
in-chief or Emperor of the Invisible Empire."

Acting in pursuance of the constitution,
which provides that the organization is "military in character," the propagation department
functions in pretty much the same manner as
the army handles its business. The Imperial
Kleagle is virtually a Chief of Staff, or more
properly an Adjutant General. The country is
divided into eight "Domains" comprising certain States, each State being known as a

"Realm," which is again divided into districts where the actual field work is done.

The "Domain" is in command of a "Grand Goblin," the "Realm" is under the jurisdiction of a "King Kleagle," while the field organizer, having charge of certain territory, is known as a "Kleagle."

The following is 'a list of the Domains with their respective Grand Goblins, revised to July 2, 1921:

1. Domain of the Southeast, composed of Georgia, Tennessee, Virginia, Alabama, Mississippi and the two Carolinas, with M. B. Owen, Box 1472, Atlanta, as Grand Goblin.

2. Western Domain, in charge of Grand Goblin George B. Kimbro, Jr., Box 1521, Houston, Texas, and composed of Arizona, Arkansas, Texas, Oklahoma, Louisiana, New Mexico, Colorado, Utah, Wyoming and Montana.

3. Domain of the East, Grand Goblin Lloyd P. Hooper, Apartment 1, No. 320, Central Park West, New York City, in charge, composed of the State of New York.

4. Domain of the Great Lakes, in charge of Grand Goblin C. W. Love, with headquarters in Chicago, and composed of Wisconsin, Illinois, Indiana, Kentucky, Ohio, Minnesota and Michigan.

5. Domain of the Mississippi Valley, in charge of Grand Goblin Frank A. Crippen, Box 951, St. Louis, composed of Nebraska,

Missouri, Kansas, Iowa, Minnesota, South Dakota and North Dakota.

6. Domain of the Pacific Coast, in charge of Grand Goblin W. S. Coburn, No. 519 Haas Building, Los Angeles, composed of California, Washington, Nevada, Oregon and Idaho.

7. Domain of the Northwest, consolidated with former Southwestern Domain and now part of new Western Domain.

8. Capitol Domain, in charge of Grand Goblin Harry B. Terrell, Box 5, 11th Street Station, Washington, D. C., and comprising the District of Columbia.

9. Atlantic Domain, in charge of Grand Goblin F. W. Atkins, with headquarters in Philadelphia, composed of Pennsylvania, New Jersey, Delaware and Maryland.

10. New England Domain, in charge of Grand Goblin A. J. Pardon, Jr., with headquarters in Boston, and composed of Maine, New Hampshire, Vermont, Massachusetts and Connecticut.

Unattached, Florida, to be in charge of King Kleagle S. A. Givens, who will report direct to the Imperial Kleagle and whose address is Box 1883, Jacksonville, Fla.

These "Domains" may be likened to divisions of an army, as they are in control of the spread of Ku Kluxism in the sections named, and the "Grand Goblin" reports direct to the "Imperial Kleagle." Each State or "Realm" is like a regiment, and the King Kleagle reports to his immediate chief, the "Grand Goblin," and not to the Atlanta headquarters. The "Kleagle" or field man makes his reports to the "King Kleagle" only. All communications sent to or received by him from the headquarters come through the channels of the "King Kleagle." The system is so thoroughly military that if a member of the organization writes to Atlanta about any matter, the letter is sent through channels to the Kleagle for his action.

The Kleagle is empowered to administer the obligation, organize and instruct Klans, and collect the requisite and necessary "donation" of ten dollars. Out of this sum he retains four dollars per member for his services, and at the end of the week submits a report of his activities, remitting to the King Kleagle the six dollars balance due on each member secured. The King Kleagle retains one dollar a member for his services, and remits five dollars to the Grand Goblin of the Domain to which he is attached. The Grand Goblin is allowed to shave off fifty cents a member and remits $4.50 to the Imperial Kleagle, who in turn keeps $2.50 and pays into the treasury of the Imperial Palace the sum of $2.00 which is all of the original "donation" that actually reaches the organization. The whole system is carefully conducted as a well organized sales system, each official being required to file his returns each week on a form provided for that purpose. The following is a copy of the Kleagle's weekly report form:

KLEAGLE'S WEELKY REPORT

This report MUST be accurately made out and mailed to the Imperial Kleagle on the last day of the week, approved by him and sent by him to the Imperial Office at the earliest possible date.

To the Imperial Wizard, Knights of the Ku Klux Klan:

The following is my report for the week ending.............., 192.......

Number of Prospective Petitioners Canvassed . . . .

   "   " Petitioners Secured and Paid . . . .

   "   " "Original Klansmen" secured . . . .

   "   " Klans Organized . . . .

Total Amount Collected from Petitioners . . . . . $.............

   "   " Remitted herewith . . . . $.............

Town or Towns I have worked in this week:

....

Will be at work next week in.....................................

....

Prospects for next week..

REMARKS.

....
....
....
....
....

Dated at..................., ...192.......

    Signed:

    ....

                        K. O. I. E.

Received......................., 192.......
Approved

....   Grade.....................
     Imperial Kleagle.

N. B.—Send names and addresses of Petitioners who have paid on another sheet, also state to what Klan they will be attached

Has the "Invisible Empire" a program?

According to its "Emperor" it not only has a program, but at the proper time it will put it forth. He made a statement which was printed in the *Searchlight* on July 2, 1921:

"I am not at all surprised, at the progress of the work, but of course gratified. I have never for one moment doubted that if God gave me strength and 'men' with which to lay before America the Knights of the Ku Klux Klan, that it would sweep the nation as nothing of the kind has ever done.

"The Ku Klux Klan has not started to work. The enemies of the organization have been howling and back-biting and snapping at everything they could see or hear, and lying slanders have been spread broadcast about the organization and leaders and proposed work and present activity.

"For the edification of those who do not know allow me to say that the Ku Klux Klan have not yet started to work and may not do so for a year. We are merely organizing at the present time and we do not intend to start any definite activity until we have sufficiently organized to make sure success.

"To those who love fireworks — rhetorical and other-wise — allow me to suggest that they wait quietly until the Ku Klux Klan passes through its organizing period and actually starts work. The attacks that have so far been launched will appear significant when the atmos-phere becomes surcharged with the shrieks of the enemies of law and order, constitutional principles, and real Americanism, as these forces feel the tightening grip of the Klan around them and they come to the realization that they are whipped.

"It will be then, and not till then, that the real anathemas will be hurled at the organization and its leaders, but it will have as little weight and do as little harm as all the lies that have been spread broadcast up to the present time.

"And those who have deliberately maligned and slandered us are going to wake some day to a very unpleasant situation. We are keeping records and making plans. The day of our activity has not arrived."

This intemperate language of Simmons was even exceeded at a meeting held on the night of August 25, 1921, in Philadelphia, which was reported in a press telegram as follows:

"A narrow pathway leading to a woodland glade, and every fifty feet a masked and white-robed sentinel. Within the little clearing an altar, and beside it the banner of the nation with the night wind rustling through the folds. Formed in hollow square around the glade rank on rank of masked spectres. A deep voice echoing through the darkness.

"'Imperial One, the men who seek admission to our legions stand prepared!'

"Line after line the candidates marched in, led by a gigantic masker who bore high overhead the Fiery Cross. The candidates marched before the scrutinizing ranks of silent Klansmen. Then every man — veteran Klansmen and new-made members — bowed before the American flag and through the night boomed out the watchword of the order:

"'All men in America must honor that flag — if we must make them honor it on their knees!'

"Then, in a blaze of sudden light, the Grand Goblin of the Realm, a towering form in white and scarlet uniform, appeared at the north end of the glade. Cheers received him. His speech was brief.

"'America for real Americans!' he cried. 'Guardianship against the alien, the anarchist and all who would subvert that banner, be they white, or black or yellow!' the voice thundered through the ranks. 'The Ku Klux are misrepresented and vilified. Americans do not realize that they sleep on a red volcano's edge. They sleep; they let petty politicians hold the helm; they make no prepara ·

tions for the perils yet to come. The enemies of true American principles are myriad. They are organized; they plot; they scheme — they go unchallenged and unhindered.

"'It is the place of the Ku Klux Klan to rouse the spirit of the real American and to stand guard against the evil forces that seek to stifle this mightiest of nations. Be the foes white, black or yellow; be they native traitors or alien invaders, the Klan shall form a ring of steel to throttle their every devil's scheme. We, the Ku Klux Klan; we, the Invisible Empire, rally to aid the faltering hands of our law — and to protect our homes, our lives, our people and our nation's future against a wave of living hell!'"

CHAPTER V

PROPAGATION NEWS–LETTERS

IN order to keep the various units in touch with each other, the Propagation Department sends out each week a "News-letter" filled with extracts from reports of different workers. These letters are supposed to be read at the meetings of the Klans, and I found that they were listened to with great attention. It is quite likely that many hundreds of reports are received each week from all over the United States, and the fact that the Propagation Department selects for distribution these special extracts must indicate what the leaders wish Klansmen as a whole to believe about the movement, and what should be the objects they are to work for. It is also to be noted how well the letters reflect the extent to which the Klans have absorbed the moral and political poison of Ku Kluxism under the sugar coating of "social purity," "one hundred per cent Americanism," "motherhood," and all the other *et ceteras*. This sugar coating is especially evident in the following extract of June 18, 1921:

"At eight o'clock one hundred Klansmen in robes marched down the main street to the park. They carried banners, the first about the head of the procession, bearing the inscription, 'The Invisible Empire, here yesterday, here today, here forever.' The second banner about the middle of the procession stated, 'Rockmart Must Be Clean for Our Mothers, for Our Wives, for Our Daughters — The Guilty Must Pay.' Then came the third and last banner reading, 'White Supremacy,' and on the reverse side, 'Grafters, Gamblers and Thieves Must Go.' There were about twelve hundred gathered around the speakers' stand and the old citizens say it was about the biggest gathering ever held in Rockmart.

"The meeting was opened with singing 'My Country, 'Tis of Thee,' by the entire gathering. This was followed by prayer led by Rev. F. J. Mashburn. Then the Reverend Mashburn made the introductory speech, in which he paid his respect to those who tried to dissuade him from having anything to do with the meeting. Doctor Mashburn paid eloquent tribute to the men in robes. He said that his father was one of the members of the original Ku Klux Klan and that he felt he had been singularly honored when requested to introduce the chief speaker of the evening, Col. J. Q. Nolan of Atlanta. Colonel Nolan followed Doctor Mashburn with an eloquent address, in which he clearly and forcefully explained the aims and purposes of the order. His hold on the audience was absolute and he was frequently interrupted with applause. His tribute to motherhood was one of the sublimest word paintings ever uttered. On the platform with the speakers were Hon. J. A. Fambro, mayor of Rockmart, members of the City Council and two members of the Klan."

In another letter from an Exalted Cyclops the sugar coating has largely disappeared. The author has lost sight of the small town "purity" reflected in the above letter, but feels that he will soon be called upon to march as a crusader against the foe. He writes:

"Long live the Klan and those noble spirits who are inculcating its creed into the hearts of slumbering America! This organization happened just at the right psychological time; a little later perhaps would have been too late; it stepped into the breach at the proper moment and no other kind of organization on earth could have possibly met the issue. You know and I know and every other thinking man realizes and will admit the perils that menace this republic of ours. The trouble is, too few people are given to thinking — people nowadays are educated to every damn thing under the sun except think. It is up to us to fill the void and I believe we can put the world to thinking. It is not only the thinking man's duty to think, but to have the moral courage to teach. In due course of time I feel no doubt but that the influence of this Invisible Empire of thinkers will be reflected in the destiny of this nation. I am a Mason, a Rotarian and several other things, all of which I am proud, but first of all I am proudest of the fact that I am a native-born, white Gentile Klansman. What kind of country would this be with no lines drawn between the Caucasian blood and the African race? It is too awful to contemplate. I solemnly believe that we are facing another crisis in our history; it is slowly, gradually, inevitably and surely approaching. The foreign political and labor class fanatic; the negro; the Jap and Romanism are threatening, if I can read the signs of the times. The new, the reincarnated Ku Klux Klan is, as I understand it, dedicated to the proposition of saving our flag and forever maintaining this government as a *white man's* government. No nobler or grander cause was ever espoused by the brain and heart of man."

"Emperor" Simmons claims that the "Invisible Empire" is increasing at the rate of five thousand a week, and several extracts from the "News-letters" might seem to prove his point; if not that they might serve the purpose of the

leaders of inspiring members to believe that
they have the honor of belonging to the great
national movement of the century.

In the weekly "News-letter," dated May 13,
1921, the Exalted Cyclops, of Vicksburg, Mississippi, writes:

"You gentlemen at headquarters will probably be
pleased to know what rapid strides the K. K. K. is
making in this State. It is sweeping Mississippi like
wildfire. We are in hopes of having five hundred members in our Klan by September 1, 1921. When we get
our Klan up to one thousand members we have perfected a scheme whereby, while we will retain only one
Klan here in Warren County, we will have all the members from each separate district meet once a week and
then have a general meeting for the whole Klan each
month, as it will be too unwieldy to have such a large
body meet frequently. You can readily appreciate this
when at our first meeting, when we had one hundred and
twenty-five charter members, we had thirty-five automobiles in the grounds of our meeting place in the
country.

"The reason why everybody here has taken so keenly
to the Klan is due to the fact that years ago the Jews
and Roman Catholics formed a liaison with the liquor
interests and have had politics in this city throttled, and
it is our intention to whip and rout them at the polls
when the next election comes around in 1922. We intend
to put these un-American elements out of office precisely
as other communities have done."

The following letter from Grand Goblin
Crippen, of St. Louis is of interest:

"I am glad to report that word comes from the Realm
of Kansas that a Ku Klux flying squadron has been
formed in that State, and I would also advise that several

Klansmen are getting together a large group of musicians who, they claim, will constitute one of the largest and best brass bands in America, to be known as the Ku Klux Band."

The "News-letter" of May 27 reveals their claim that Ku Kluxism is making strong headway outside of the Southern States. I quote at length from it as follows:

"Additional proof that the Knights of the Ku Klux Klan is being welcomed with enthusiasm by the rank and file of one hundred per cent American citizens wherever our representatives go is found in the report of Hugh B. Cobb, one of the Imperial Officers, who has just returned from a trip to Missouri and other States in that territory.

"Mr. Cobb went to Joplin, Mo., especially to deliver an address by invitation of the Joplin Klan. He says he found interest in Klankraft running high and the members of the organization there are among the highest type of citizens. On his return to Atlanta, Mr. Cobb spent one day with Grand Goblin Crippen in St. Louis. He was greatly pleased with Klansman Crippen and the work he is doing for the organization.

"It is an inspiration to see the class of citizens who are knocking at the outer door and applying for citizenship in the Invisible Empire,' said Mr. Cobb. 'The best publicity or propaganda our organization can have is the criticism of its enemies. No real American citizen is deceived for long, if at all, by these critics, because when he finds out who they are the first question he naturally asks is: Why are they criticizing? And if he has any brains at all it doesn't take him long to find out.'

"Mr. Cobb's report is indeed very encouraging since it deals with the progress we are making in territory outside of the South. The red-blooded American men of the North and West are accepting the Ku Klux Klan as an American institution, because it is such, and because it is the *only* one hundred per cent American organization in the whole United States. Think it over.

"Another convincing proof that the Klan is taking hold is found in the fact that our enemies are so rapidly attacking us. We mean something to them apparently, although they scoffed at us in the beginning. There is very little scoffing going on at the present time, but there is considerable gnashing of teeth. We are glad to say, however, that the bulk of the opposition with which we are meeting now comes from those from whom we naturally would expect opposition and with whom it is impossible for the Ku Klux Klan ever to have anything in common.

"At the outset we were opposed by many newspapers who had no idea of our real aims and purposes. *They accepted the word of negro associations and Catholics, Jews and other foreigners that we were a lawless gang and criticized us accordingly.*"

There is considerable food for thought in the above extract. In the first place I have never heard, in an experience of nearly twenty years, of a fraternal order sending out a communication in which it designated the outside public or any part of it as "enemies."

It will be noted in several of the "News-letters" that one of the points I am trying to bring out in my argument is confirmed. It is the classification of the white Catholic and the white Jew with the negro, a classification that can have but one inevitable effect — the creating of discord and dissension among members of the white race.

The last "News-letter" I have read was the one dated June 25. It was read at a meeting I attended in Chattanooga, and was descriptive

principally of the work being done on the
Pacific Coast by Grand Goblin Coburn, who
has charge of that Domain. The report indicated that a vigorous propagation campaign
was going on in California and that people
were eagerly joining the Ku Klux Klan in
response to its appeal for membership on the
ground of "white supremacy" over the Japanese. I fully believe that the Pacific Coast will
become one of the strongholds of Ku Kluxism,
and would not be surprised at any time to read
in the newspapers of some surface manifesta-
tions of the agitation of the race question.
That a movement managed in Atlanta, Ga.,
has no business meddling in the international
affairs of this country is so obvious that it is
quite unnecessary to comment further upon it.

The manner in which applications for membership are solicited in connection with the
work of the official lecturers is illustrated in
the following description of a lecture:

"At the regular meeting of the Newport News Klan
No. 8, Realm of Virginia, held in its Klavern, Monday,
May 30, a resolution was introduced and passed by
unanimous vote that Your Majesty be requested if
possible to return Col. J. Q. Nolan to Newport News at
a future date to deliver another address. Colonel Nolan
spoke at the Imperial Theater with a seating capacity of
eight hundred with the standing room only sign displayed
before he even began speaking. There were fully as many
turned away as were able to hear him. If possible to
have him return we will secure the Academy of Music
for his address and we can promise him a packed house.
Colonel Nolan won the hearts of all who heard him and

the request for his return comes not only from Klansmen but from men and women from all walks of life. At the meeting following Colonel's Nolan's address, ninety-one applications were presented and interest has been aroused to fever heat here. If it can be made possible for Colonel Nolan to return, please have him do so. At the same time we would like to extend a warm personal invitation to Your Majesty to come with Colonel Nolan, for Newport News and our Klan would feel it an honor indeed to entertain Your Majesty."

Several of the "News-letters" support my claim that the organization is endeavoring to throw its coils around all public officers. This is seen for instance in the letter of May 20, 1921, which reads:

"You may state in your weekly letter that in one city in Virginia we have the chief of police, the commonwealth attorney, the postmaster, the police court judge, members of the city council and the managing editor of the leading paper and many other prominent business and professional men. This is Newport News."

The "News-letter" of June 10, 1921, shows a still more sinister situation. The Exalted Cyclops of Norfolk, Virginia, writes:

"We have just taken in the chief of police. He is a fine up-standing fellow, a major in the World War. We had a hard time getting information regarding him, but when we found that he was eligible we had no trouble enlisting him in our ranks and when he was initiated you never saw such a pleased fellow; he radiated it, and when he learned he was to have our support in upholding the law he was certainly pleased, especially with our military organization, which we offered him in case of trouble. He then informed us that the city is insufficiently pro-

tected and that we are sitting on a volcano regarding the
negro question, that there is a great deal of unrest among
them and that we might have a riot at any time and he
was very much worried. He told us that not many
months ago there was a riot in the negro district, caused
by negro soldiers attacking a district police station to
release a negro prisoner, but it never got into the papers
— so it was news to all of us. He welcomed us and the
military company is to be trained and two hundred and
sixty repeating rifles will be turned over to us in time of
trouble. I asked how many in the three hundred present
at the meeting would be willing to join the organization
to assist the chief, and every one of them stood up.
How is that for one hundred per cent Americanism?
They were told they might have to sacrifice their lives in
case of trouble, but they did not flinch at duty. The
chief of police states that any man we select to head these
two hundred and sixty Klansmen will be made by him
assistant director of public safety in charge of these
Klansmen."

Imperial Kleagle Clarke, commenting on the
above communication, states: "We call that
almighty fine. The Norfolk Klan is working
along the right line and deserves to be highly
commended for the steps it has taken in
enforcement of the law and preservation of
order."

An examination of the Norfolk communication reveals some interesting points. In the first
place the author of the letter says: "We had a
hard time getting information regarding him,
but when we found that he was eligible we had
no trouble enlisting him in our ranks." In
other words, some of the best and most efficient police officers in the United States are

Irish-Catholics, and since, according to the
Ku Klux Klan, they are foreigners and to be
classed with the negro, it is highly important,
first of all, to ascertain the religion of the chief
of police. As he probably is not an active church-
goer this task was rather difficult, but when he
was found to be a Protestant, he was eagerly
sought after. Now that the chief has taken the
oath of allegiance to the "Invisible Empire,"
and has surrounded himself with his two hundred and sixty Ku Kluxes, I would not give
much for the chances of a Catholic to get on
the Norfolk police force. It is also interesting
to read the fact that this particular Klan states
that it is military, and that a military company
will be trained and drilled, and that rifles will
be issued to this secret organization. If this is a
straw indicating the way in which the Ku Klux
wind is blowing, it is not unreasonable to suppose that in the course of time there will be a
gigantic, secret, national organization drilled as
soldiers, and under the autocratic command of
the "Emperor of the Invisible Empire."

The "News-letter" above quoted again makes
an extract from the report of the Exalted
Cyclops of the Norfolk Klan, which is really
more dangerous to the United States than the
one previously discussed. It is more dangerous
for the reason that it reflects the insane light
of religious fervor and fanaticism in connection with this movement, and shows how the
attempt of Simmons to build a secret Empire

on the religious idea is bearing its fruit. I
bespeak for this effusion a careful reading:

"I did not think it possible that my enthusiasm for
our noble order could be increased, but your letter of the
fourteenth instant, has filled me with added inspiration.
Having been offered an opportunity for service in the
field in Missouri, I am resigning my position with the
government here and hope soon to be among the chosen
disciples of our great Emperor proclaiming his inspired
doctrine of new freedom to the world. Beyond the simple
office of treasurer in my home county I have never
sought public honors nor craved political preference, but
in the glorious work of this God-inspired order every
ounce of my energy will strive for excellence. I shall
never seek the honor or preferment of office except
wherein I may contribute to the honor and preferment of
my Klan. My fellow Klansmen have here seen fit to
confer upon me the highest honor within their power,
and God being my witness, I would not barter it for any
other honor that life may hold. My only consolation in
leaving my faithful Klan for a time is that I may aid in
the promulgation of the glorious institutions of freedom
which my sons battled for beneath the Stars and Stripes
for which I have pledged my blood beneath the flaming
symbol of an unconquered race of men."

These "News-letters" are valuable as showing the mental attitude of the workers and members of the Ku Klux Klan. They show that
wherever it is possible the national organization
desires to throw its net around the officers of
the law, and enroll them in the system. Under
the guise of assisting the authorities to enforce
the law this is done, and to my personal knowledge many conscientious and capable officers
of the law believe that the idea is a good one.

At the same time it is an alarming situation when police officers and sheriffs who have already taken one oath to the States in which they reside, take another — a vicious and illegal obligation — to an "Invisible Empire," ruled autocratically by one man who has in mind plans he does not reveal to his followers. What is to happen when the chief of police of a city swears to obey "unconditionally" all laws, regulations, decrees and edicts of the Ku Klux Klan "which have been or which may be hereafter enacted."

Whatever excuse the original Ku Klux Klan may have had for its existence, it is impossible to conceive any situation arising in this country at the present time that calls for any extra-judicial organization, functioning in secret, and composed of men wearing robes and masks to conceal their identities. And along this line, I want to call attention to a historical fact. The original Klan was organized and functioned at a time when the courts and law-enforcing machinery of the South were paralyzed, but, as soon as the courts began to administer justice, General Forrest, the Grand Wizard, of the Ku Klux Klan, issued an order disbanding the organization on the ground that it was no longer needed. Surely, if the original Klan, having functioned as an enormous "vigilance committee" in several States, found that its services were not required, what real excuse can be advanced for the continuance of an extra-judicial organization in these days of ample courts, able officers of the law and the administration of justice? It seems to me that there are more than enough law-enforcement agencies in the United States.

If the system of judicature in the United States is so helpless that a secret, masked, "Invisible Empire" is necessary to enforce the law, then the cold truth is that the Federal and State governments are abject failures. This then, being the case, it should be the duty of the people to devise ways and means to create and maintain a new system. In the face of the fact that this country has grown from a few small colonies to one of the greatest of world powers, and that the Constitution of the United States has been the basic law under which this has been done, and that our system of law enforcement is entirely adequate, the attempt on the part of any organization whatever to take upon itself the enforcement of the law is a piece of presumptuous impudence. All laws are made and enforced by representatives of the whole people. They are not enacted by or for the benefit of a class and they cannot be enforced by a class.

The "News-letters" also indicate that the teachings of Simmons are taking firm root in the minds of the religious element of the country. While I may be disputed on this point, I believe, from my observations in various sections of the country which I have visited,

that the people of the South as a whole take
their churches and their religions more seriously
than do people elsewhere. The whole structure
of modern Ku Kluxism is an attempt to clothe
its real purposes and intentions in the garb of
the backwoods religious revival. Its ritualism is
of the camp-meeting order, and all its ceremonies, as I shall show later, tend to awaken
the emotions of provincial Protestantism. History has shown in numerous instances that where
this religious fervor is aroused, it produces a
blind fanaticism that is one of the most dangerous forces in the body politic when it is turned
loose. The inability of the fanatic to differ-
entiate between the political activities of the
Roman Catholic Hierarchy and the Roman Catholic Church as a great religious institution is
one of the greatest menaces of the Ku Klux
movement.

The "News-letters" show further that already
the fanatical "citizens" of the "Invisible
Empire" are catching hold of the idea of
autocracy, and that the "subjects" are addressing their rulers as "Your Majesty."

Were the situation not so serious and of such
vital moment to the American people, this
"Empire" of Ku Kluxism would be one of the
greatest pieces of humor ever perpetrated upon
the American public.

CHAPTER VI

THE KU KLUX OATH

In the printed literature of the "Invisible Empire," it is stated that those who cannot assume a "real oath," with serious determination to keep same inviolate, are not desired in the ranks of Ku Kluxism. There is no doubt whatever that "Emperor" Simmons, who probably wrote the oath, has produced a "real oath."

In making a critical analysis of the oath, I shall first reproduce it in its entirety, and then take it up in sections and show my viewpoint. If this oath is not a dangerous document and likely to imbue people with the spirit of taking the law into their own hands, then a considerable portion of my contention against the Ku Klux Klan must necessarily fail. My case against Ku Kluxism rests to a large extent upon the potential danger to the country from an absolutely secret organization, bound together by this oath, under the sole domination of one man, and likely at any time to draw into its ranks men with no regard for anything but the Ku Klux law.

The oath is printed separately from the ritual, and the name "Ku Klux Klan" does not appear in it. In places where the name is spoken there are asterisks. The document consists of three printed pages bound together, and, for the convenience of the person administering it, is broken up into phrases separated by dashes. I am giving it here properly punctuated so that the reader can more easily grasp its significance. It is supposed to be administered in sections, sandwiched in between the verbose and long-winded effusions of "Emperor" Simmons as contained in the ritual. When the work is conferred by a full-degree team, it is given in "long form" and the procedure follows the order laid down in the ritual. Most of the Kleagles, however, put on the ceremony of "naturalization" alone, using the short form, in which case the oath is administered all at once. In the present mad scramble for commissions on the "donations," the Kleagles administer the obligation at any time and place that suits the convenience of the "alien" with the ten dollars, and Ku Kluxes are manufactured on the "pay-as-you-enter" style in stores, factories, banks, physicians' offices and any other place where there is freedom from intrusion. One enthusiastic Kleagle wrote to the home office that he had arisen from his bed one night after midnight, and clad in his pajamas had administered the obligation to a "worthy alien," whose ten dollars burned so badly in his pocket that he could not wait until daylight to be separated from his money.

The obligation, consisting of four sections, reads as follows:

"Section I. Obedience.

"(You will say) 'I' (pronounce your full name — and repeat after me) —'In the presence of God and man most solemnly pledge, promise, and swear, unconditionally, that I will faithfully obey the Constitution and laws; and will willingly conform to all regulations, usages, and requirements of the Knights of the Ku Klux Klan, which do now exist or which may be hereafter enacted; and will render at all times loyal respect and steadfast support to the Imperial Authority of same; and will heartily heed all official mandates, decrees, edicts, rulings, and instructions of the Imperial Wizard thereof. I will yield prompt response to all summonses, I having knowledge of same, Providence alone preventing.

" Section II. Secrecy.

"I most solemnly swear that I will forever keep sacredly secret the signs, words, and grip; and any and all other matters and knowledge of the Knights of the Ku Klux Klan, regarding which a most rigid secrecy must be maintained, which may at any time be communicated to me and will never divulge same nor even cause the same to be divulged to any person in the whole world, unless I know positively that such person is a member of this Order in good and regular standing, and not even then unless it be for the best interest of this Order.

"I most sacredly vow and most positively swear that I will not yield to bribe, flattery, threats, passion, punishment, persuasion, nor any enticements whatever coming from or offered by any person or persons, male or female, for the purpose of obtaining from me a secret or secret information of the Knights of the Ku Klux Klan. I will die rather than divulge same. So help me, God. Amen!

" Section III. Fidelity.

"(You will say) 'I' (pronounce your full name — and repeat after me)—'Before God, and in the presence of these mysterious Klansmen, on my sacred honor, do most solemnly and sincerely pledge, promise, and swear that I will diligently guard, and faithfully foster every interest of the Knights of the Ku Klux Klan, and will maintain its social cast and dignity.

"I swear that I will not recommend any person for membership in this order whose mind is unsound, or whose reputation I know to be bad, or whose character is doubtful or whose loyalty to our country is in any way questionable.

"I swear that I will pay promptly all just and legal demands made upon me to defray the expenses of my Klan and this Order, when same are due or called for.

"I swear that I will protect the property of the Knights of the Ku Klux Klan, of any nature whatsoever; and if any should be intrusted to my keeping, I will properly keep or rightly use same; and will freely and promptly surrender same on official demand, or if ever I am banished from or voluntarily discontinue my membership in this Order.

"I swear that I will, most determinedly, maintain peace and harmony in all the deliberations of the gatherings or assemblies of the Invisible Empire, and of any subordinate jurisdiction or Klan thereof.

"I swear that I will most strenuously discourage selfishness and selfish political ambition on the part of myself or any Klansman.

"I swear that I will never allow personal friendship, blood or family relationship, nor personal, political or professional prejudice, malice, or ill will, to influence me in casting my vote for the election or rejection of an applicant for membership in this Order, God being my Helper. AMEN!

"SECTION IV. KLANISHNESS.

"(You will say) 'I' (pronounce your full name — and repeat after me) —'Most solemnly pledge, promise, and swear that I will never slander, defraud, deceive, or in any manner wrong the Knights of the Ku Klux Klan, a

Klansman, nor a Klansman's family, nor will I suffer the same to be done, if I can prevent it.

"I swear that I will be faithful in defending and protecting the home, reputation, and physical and business interest of a Klansman and that of a Klansman's family.

"I swear that I will at any time, without hesitating, go to the assistance or rescue of a Klansman in any way; at his call I will answer; I will be truly Klanish toward Klansmen in all things honorable.

"I swear that I will not allow any animosity, friction, nor ill will to arise and remain between myself and a Klansman; but will be constant in my efforts to promote real Klanishness among the members of this Order.

"I swear that I will keep secure to myself a secret of a Klansman when same is committed to me in the sacred bond of Klansmanship — the crime of violating *this* solemn oath, treason against the United States of America, rape, and malicious murder, alone excepted.

"I most solemnly assert and affirm that to the government of the United States of America and any State thereof which I may become a resident, I sacredly swear an unqualified allegiance above any other and every kind of government in the whole world. I, here and now, pledge my life, my property, my vote, and my sacred honor, to uphold its flag, its constitution, and constitutional laws; and will protect, defend, and enforce same to death.

"I swear that I will most zealously and valiantly shield and preserve, by any and all justifiable means and methods, the sacred constitutional rights and privileges of free public schools, free speech, free press, separation of church and state, liberty, white supremacy, just laws, and the pursuit of happiness, against any encroachment, of any nature, by any person or persons, political party or parties, religious sect or people, native, naturalized, or foreign of any race, color, creed, lineage, or tongue whatsoever.

"All, to which I have sworn by *this* oath, I will seal with my blood. Be thou my witness, Almighty God! Amen!"

This document is the oath of the "Invisible Empire," Knights of the Ku Klux Klan, and according to "Emperor" Simmons, good Americans are swearing to it at the rate of five thousand a week! For the benefit of those who cannot readily see the danger in such an obligation, and why it does not belong in the class of obligations assumed by men who join real fraternal orders, let us carefully analyze certain clauses.

"SECTION I. OBEDIENCE.

"I, in the presence of God and man, most solemnly pledge, promise, and swear, unconditionally, that I will faithfully obey the Constitution and laws; and will willingly conform to all regulations, usages, and requirements of the Knights of the Ku Klux Klan, which do now exist or which may be hereafter enacted; and will render at all times loyal respect and steadfast support to the Imperial Authority of same; and will heartily heed all official mandates, decrees, edicts, rulings, and instructions of the Imperial Wizard thereof. I will yield prompt response to all summonses, I having knowledge of same, Providence alone preventing.

Until I had resigned as Kleagle I had never been able to even see a copy of the constitution and laws. This was in the possession of the King Kleagle of Tennessee, who stated that he had had great difficulty in securing it, and had been compelled to give a very rigid receipt for its care and custody. The organization was evidently afraid to allow this booklet to get into general circulation among the members, for the simple reason that its general perusal would have shown the members the truth. They would have discovered that the organization was a "one-man" affair, with "Emperor" Simmons in practical control, with a life-time easy job, living on "Easy Street" as a result of money that came into the organization from the public. They would also have found that they were members of a military organization, and that the "Emperor" was the Commander-in-chief. Obedience to the "Imperial Authority" means obedience to "Emperor" Simmons.

This first section binds a "citizen" to obey "unconditionally" laws he has never seen and is not permitted to see, and also to obey all laws that may be enacted in the future regardless of whether he approves of the laws or not. Any man who takes this obligation and keeps it, gives "Emperor" William Joseph Simmons a blank check on his life, his liberty of thought, and his entire actions. Any one who doubts my statement has but to read this section of the oath. It is there in plain English. Regardless of the merits of the organization, no fraternal order man ought to be a member of any society in which he has so little voice in the management of its affairs, and the head of which has so framed the constitution that he will enjoy a lifetime of "easy money." And the incorporators of the "Invisible Empire" say in their application for a charter of the "Knights of the Ku Klux Klan" that they want to be classed with the Masons and Knights of Pythias! In both those orders, the constitution and laws of the order are always open for the inspection of any member who cares to see them, and I have yet to hear of an official of Pythianism or Masonry who has been chosen to hold a position for life. Some officials have held office on merit for many years, but their tenure for life is not fixed in the constitutions.

Under the second section of the oath, in the first clause, is found the words:

"I . . . do most solemnly pledge, promise and swear, that I will diligently guard and faithfully foster every interest of the Knights of the Ku Klux Klan, and will maintain its social cast and dignity."

This is a sweeping declaration that every interest of this organization must be held paramount, and the slightest deviation from absolute obedience and loyalty to "Emperor" Simmons, who is the organization, would mean that the offender had broken his oath. "Maintaining its social cast and dignity"— whatever that means — may indeed be a very hard obligation to keep.

"I swear that I will pay promptly all just and legal demands made upon me to defray the expenses of my Klan and this Order, when same are due or called for."

Here we find that the avarice and greed that permeates the whole system of organized Ku Kluxism has even been incorporated into the oath. When a Klan is chartered, a per capita tax of $1.85 for each member is required to be sent to the Imperial Palace. If the organization has 650,000 members, as has been claimed, then there will be derived from dues alone an annual revenue of $1,202,500. In order to insure the payment of this vast sum, the "Emperor" has sworn all his "subjects" to keep up the golden stream that flows into the coffers of the "Invisible Empire." Under this section, it would also be possible to levy an assessment on all of the members, which they would be bound to pay, or else they would be guilty of violating their obligations. No amount of payment is specified. When a person assumes the obligation, he gives "Emperor" Simmons a blank check on his bank account.

"I swear that I will never allow personal friendship, blood or family relationship, nor personal, political, or professional prejudice, malice, or ill will, to influence me in casting my vote for the election or rejection of an applicant for membership in this Order."

The "Invisible Empire" wants more "citizens." More "citizens" mean more money. Under a ruling of the organization no person can be blackballed unless objectors are prepared to stand up in open lodge and state just what are their objections, and then they might be admonished to "lay off." In the present system of propagation the Kleagle is the court of last resort as to the persons who become charter members of a Klan.

Much capital is made by the organization of the fact that each person who becomes a "citi-

zen" of the "Invisible Empire" is required to
take a solemn oath to support the Constitution
of the United States. While this is true, the
allegiance to the Constitution and the law, is,
in my opinion, pure camouflage for the purpose
of concealing the deadly fangs of this illegal
oath. In considering this point, it should be
borne in mind that the members of the original
Ku Klux Klan also took an oath to support the
Constitution of the United States, which oath
can be found in the Prescript of the Order.
Just how much weight the original Ku Kluxes
attached to the Constitution of the United States
when it became necessary to put the fear of
God into a "carpet-bagger" or negro is a
matter of more or less doubt. They were organized as a matter of necessity for the purpose of
policing a section of the country where political
madness and hatred reigned supreme. As will
be shown further along, a Ku Klux Klan in
Beaumont, Texas, in May, 1921, although all
of its members had sworn to support the Constitution of the United States, arrested a citizen
without a warrant, tried him with a jury, convicted him, and acted as his executioners in
total violating of the Bill of Rights of the
United States Constitution. It has been proven
in one instance that swearing allegiance to the
United States Constitution had but little effect
in preventing members of the "Invisible Empire"
from committing acts of lawlessness. Hence, I
believe that the pious and patriotic clause in

the oath of "Emperor" Simmons' organization
is sheer camouflage, because the very document
shows on its face that the Ku Klux oath is
considered paramount to any other tie or obligation.

In order to prove this latter statement, I
call special attention to the following clause,
which illustrates fully the relative importance
the "Invisible Empire" attaches to the Constitution of the United States and the Ku Klux
obligation:

"I swear that I will keep secure to myself a secret of a
Klansman, when same is committed to me in the sacred
bond of Klansmanship — the crime of violating *this*
solemn oath, treason against the United States of America,
rape, and malicious murder, alone excepted."

Note this clause well! "The crime of violating *this* solemn oath" comes first! Treason
against the United States of America, rape and
murder are afterthoughts. Under this clause, a
Klansman can go to another Klansman and
confess to having committed robbery, seduction,
burglary and nearly every other crime in the
calendar, and the one to whom the commission
of the crime was confessed would be bound to
keep the information secure to himself. But,
however, if a Klansman should confess to one
of his fellows that he had broken his Ku Klux
oath, that violation of the obligation is a crime
of so heinous a nature that it is of more importance to the Ku Klux mind than the crime of

treason against the United States of America,
which crime comes second.

The most deadly part of the oath is saved for
the end. The candidate has been led up to it
by high-sounding words about "Klanishness,"
and has sworn allegiance to the Constitution of
the United States of America. "Emperor"
Simmons knew very well that had he started off
his oath with this clause, most of his victims
would have backed out, so he tacked it on at
the end. It reads:

"I swear that I will most zealously and valiantly shield
and preserve, by any and all justifiable means and
methods, the sacred constitutional rights and privileges
of free public schools, free speech, free press, separation
of church and state, liberty, white supremacy, just laws,
and the pursuit of happiness, against any encroachment,
of any nature, by any person or persons, political party
or parties, religious sect or people, native, naturalized,
or foreign of any race, color, creed, lineage, or tongue
whatsoever."

My contention is that this part of the obligation is absolutely illegal, that it is an accessory
before the fact to lawlessness and mob violence,
and brands the entire proposition as an outlaw
enterprise that should be abolished and suppressed by the United States and State governments. Let us study a few of the words, as
they stand out so strikingly. "Zealously and
valiantly," "shield and preserve," "any and
all justifiable means and methods," "against
any encroachment," "of any nature," "any person or persons," "political party or parties,"

"religious sect or people," "native, naturalized,
or foreign," "any race, color, lineage, or tongue
whatsoever"! Just read these groups of words
over and over again! When individuals or a
group of individuals proceed to "zealously and
valiantly" use "any and all justifiable means
and methods" to accomplish a certain specified
end, they take the law into their own hands.
When the Barons wrested Magna Charta from
King John at Runnymede, they "used any
and all justifiable means and methods"! When
the Germans invaded Belgium, and cynically
declared that a treaty was a "scrap of paper,"
they used "any and all justifiable means and
methods"! When a mob of masked outlaws
takes a helpless old man from his bed and beats
him up, they use "any and all justifiable means
and methods"! When masked men drive up to
a hotel and seize a helpless woman, convey her
to a secluded spot, strip her clothing from her
body and cover her with tar and feathers, they
have used "any and all justifiable means and
methods." Under this outrageous oath, any
band of ruffians or outlaws can defend any
lawless action they wish to commit on the
ground that the "means and methods" were
"justifiable."

In the concrete instance I have previous
mentioned, where the *Johnson City Staff* under-
took to protest against the coming of Ku Kluxism to the town, the spirit of the "Invisible
Empire" interpreted "freedom of speech" to

mean freedom only in so far as the Ku Klux
Klan was allowed to proceed with its affairs
unmolested. As soon as opposition developed
the Ku Klux "freedom of the press" manifested itself in a desire to boycott the newspaper. Under the obligation to use "any and
all justifiable means and methods" I see no
reason to deter a local organization from taking
an editor out and administering a liberal coating of tar and feathers, in case he should presume,
in the columns of his paper, to antagonize the
"Invisible Empire."

I have been a student of the Constitution of
the United States for twenty years, but until I
saw the oath of the Ku Klux Klan, I never
knew before that "white supremacy" was a
"sacred constitutional right." The Fourteenth
and Fifteenth Amendments to the Federal
Constitution removed all political barriers
against "race, color, and previous condition of
servitude," and guaranteed all citizens of the
United States equal protection under the laws.
The Ku Klux oath, on the other hand, binds its
followers to "use any and all justifiable means
and methods" to enforce "white supremacy,"
and I see no reason why members of the organization would not interpret it to excuse any
and every shade of mob violence, lynching,
hanging, or burning of negroes.

By the term "separation of church and state"
is usually meant the resistance to the advance
of the Catholic people in the political affairs of

the country. Preachers of Protestant Churches
may get up in their pulpits and talk politics,
may make speeches on the stump, and may
take upon themselves the general duties of
running a community, but their actions are
seldom criticized. The advance of the Catholics
in politics, however, is a "union of church and
state," in the popular conception, and this
advance, the Ku Klux swears that he will resist
by "any and all justifiable means and methods."
The methods may be lawful and they may not
be, but to the "Invisible Empire's" obligation
they would be "justifiable" if they succeeded
in driving the Catholics out of public life.

It would also be well to note the blanket
phrase "the pursuit of happiness." The oath
says "use any and all justifiable means and
methods" to secure the "pursuit of happiness,"
which, by the way, is also classed as a "sacred
Constitutional right." This covers a multitude
of things. A Ku Klux might derive unbounded
happiness out of covering his neighbor's body
with tar and feathers, while the victim of the
performance might become a most unhappy
individual as a result of the operation. The
oath means in a few words that whatever suits
the Ku Klux mind, whatever it wants to do in
a community, it is going to use "any and all
justifiable means and methods" to accomplish.
The midnight prowler in his mask and white
robe might well ask the question: "What does a
little thing like a police force and sheriff's posse
matter. If they attempt to interfere with us,

we will simply remember our Ku Klux obligation, and 'zealously and valiantly shield and preserve our pursuit of happiness by any and all justifiable means and methods.' "

Under this section, any sort of crime can be excused in the mind of the person who commits the crime. "But," the answer probably will be, "an act is not justifiable unless it is legal." The obligation might easily have been written so that the distinction could have been clearly stated, but it was not. That oath on its face is an accessory before the fact to any and all kinds of crimes and outrages, and placing such an obligation indiscriminately in the hands of men of average intelligence is like giving dynamite to little children and expecting them not to be blown to pieces.

In summarizing the oath of the "Invisible Empire," there are three salient things that stand out very prominently:

First: It binds men to obey unconditionally laws they know nothing about, and laws which will be enacted in the future, and to follow blindly an organization which is largely a one-man affair.

Second: It places the Ku Klux obligation prior to the obligation to the government of the United States.

Third: Its last paragraph is illegal, and is nothing more or less than the condonement of mob rule and the use of methods in carrying out its views that are contrary to all the basic laws of the land.

CHAPTER VII

THE KU KLUX RITUAL

THIS chapter might well be entitled "Ku-Kluxing a Sacrament," or "How the Kleagles, for Ten Dollars, profane Christianity's Holiest Rite."

On the title page of the fifty-four page booklet is the imprint "Copyright 1916, by W. J. Simmons, Atlanta, Ga."

I venture to express the opinion that this is the first time in the history of the United States that a ritual of a secret order, genuine or alleged, has ever been copyrighted, and the very fact that it *is* copyrighted suggests pertinent questions. As a general rule the protection of the copyright laws is a matter of dollars and cents to an author, and the first question that suggests itself is: what royalty does Simmons get from the "Invisible Empire" for the use of his printed productions? Then comes the further question: in whom does the title to the copyright rest? does Simmons own it, or has it been assigned to the corporation? If Simmons owns the copyright, and should die, would the title to the ritual pass to his heirs or would the members of the Klan have anything to say as to the ownership of the secret book of their

organization? If the question be answered in
the negative the curious spectacle would be
presented of an organization paying a royalty
to people not members of that organization.
Another consideration is the fact that as the
law requires two copies of a book to be deposited
in the Library of Congress, the pages of this
"secret" document are open to the study of
any one who cares to go to Washington to
examine them. Therefore, in his desire to secure
unto himself the property rights in the ritual,
Simmons, who took the oath not to divulge
any of the secrets of his organization, violated
his obligation from the very beginning. As I
am no longer a member of the Knights of the
Ku Klux Klan, I have no interest whatever in
the relations of Simmons to his organization,
but merely suggest these questions for the benefit of the members who may be interested in
the financial side of their own movement.

The name of the Ku Klux ritual is the
"Kloran."

Before discussing this name, which has an
interesting story, it is necessary to state that
in all of the Ku Klux lingo, many words have
been formed by the placing of the letter "L"
after the first letter of a word. Thus we have
"Klavern," the meeting place of the Klan,
from "Kavern;" Kloncilium, from Koncilium;
Klaliff, from Kaliff, etc., etc. The name "Kloran" is the word "Koran" with the letter "L"
placed after the "K."

The Knights of the Ku Klux Klan is an "Invisible Empire" composed of none but Protestant Christians, yet it appropriates the name of the Mohammedan Bible for its sacred book.

The "Kloran" is called the "white book," and on its front cover bears the inscription "K-Uno," from which is inferred that it is the first degree of Ku Kluxism. There is a hint in the "sacred and inspired" pages that there are other degrees to be taken, after the member has thoroughly imbibed the pages of the "Kloran," and has passed an examination upon the same. What these "higher degrees" are, no man, as far as I can learn, knows save only him, who "for fourteen years" communed with the gods and prepared himself for the sublime mission of saving the United States from nearly half of its own citizens.

On the inside cover is the "Ku Klux Kreed" which is borrowed from the creed of the original Klan, with such further additions as Simmons in his infinite wisdom saw fit to add, and this is followed by the "order of business," which is similar to the average secret order, but expressed "Simmonsly" and not in the usual plain language of other organizations.

The officers of the Klan as then set forth are "The Exalted Cyclops," who corresponds to the President; the "Klaliff," to the Vice-President; "Klokard," the lecturer; "Kludd," the Chaplain (borrowed, by the way, from the

name of the high priest of the ancient Druids);
the "Kligrapp," the Secretary; the "Klabee,"
the Treasurer; the "Kladd," the conductor;
the "Klarogo," the inner guard; the "Klexter,"
the outer guard; the "Klokann," the investigating committee; and the "Night-hawk," who
has charge of candidates.

The text of the "Kloran" starts off with an
"Imperial Decree" written in the "Simmons"
language, and signed by "His Majesty," telling
the members that this book is "*the* book" of the
"Invisible Empire," and that the decree to
preserve it, and study its sacred teachings is as
binding as the original obligation. Then follows a complicated diagram of the "Klavern,"
or meeting-place, showing the stations of the
numerous officers and the routes taken by candidates when going through the floor work.

The "opening ceremony," which is supposed
to be inflicted upon the Klan every time it
meets, covers eight closely printed pages of the
"Kloran," and is filled with tiresome and boring
conversation between the various officers. An
opening "klode," to the tune of "Greenland's
Icy Mountains," with its chorus "Home, Sweet
Home" is then to be sung, and this is followed
by a long-winded prayer ending with a petition
to the Lord to "bless our Emperor." After
more words, the poor Klan at last finds itself
open.

Then follows the "closing ceremony" which
contains five pages of the same sort of wordy

discourse, with a verse to the tune of "Blest be
the Tie that Binds," a prayer for the success of
the "Invisible Empire," and the weary Klansmen are then allowed to go home.

The bulk of the "Kloran" is taken up with
the "ceremony of naturalization." In the entire
ritual the alleged fraternal order is called the
"Invisible Empire," with only an occasional
reference to its legal incorporated title. The
candidate is an "alien" until he has been bored
to death to the extent of about thirty pages,
whereupon he is made "a citizen" of the "Invisible Empire" through the process of "naturalization." It is rather a curious anomaly that an
American citizen, who does not need to be
naturalized to enjoy the privileges of American
citizenship has to be "naturalized" as a Ku
Klux, while the foreign born, the Catholics and
the Jews cannot be naturalized at all. They are
forever "aliens."

The ceremony of naturalization consists in
walking the candidate from station to station,
causing him to listen to verbose passages,
swearing him to the obligation previously
referred to, threatening him with death if he
ever reveals any of the secrets, and finally
making him go through a parody on the solemn
and sacred rite of baptism.

As a matter of comparison with the original
Prescript of the Old Ku Klux Klan, there are
ten questions which are asked the "alien" upon
his first entrance into the "outer Den" of the

"Klavern." These ten questions unmistakably
show an intention on the part of the "Invisible
Empire" to turn the United States in a
country controlled by a "class" as opposed to
several "classes," and are so utterly at variance
with the requirements of the original Ku Klux
Klan, as to add stronger proof that the present
organization is a historical fraud with no right
to use even the name of the former organization. These questions which can be found on
pages 25 and 26 of the "Kloran" are as
follows:

"1. Is the motive prompting your ambition to be a
Klansman serious and unselfish?

"2. Are you a native born, white, Gentile American
citizen?

"3. Are you absolutely opposed to and free of any
allegiance of any nature to any cause, government,
people, sect or ruler that is foreign to the United States
of America?

"4. Do you believe in the tenets of the Christian
religion?

"5. Do you esteem the United States of America and its
institutions above any other government, civil, political
or ecclesiastical, in the whole world?

"6. Will you, without mental reservation, take a solemn
oath to defend, preserve and enforce same?

"7. Do you believe in clanishness and will you faithfully
practice same toward Klansmen?

"8. Do you believe in and will you faithfully strive for
the eternal maintenance of white supremacy?

"9. Will you faithfully obey our constitution and laws,
and conform willingly to all our usages, requirements and
regulations?

"10. Can you always be depended on?"

In the above questions, the references to the Jew and the negro are obvious. The third question, "Are you absolutely opposed to and free of any allegiance of any nature to any cause, government, sect, people or ruler that is foreign to the United States of America?" refers to the Catholic, in which the Pope is considered a foreign ruler, and the allegiance mentioned means spiritual allegiance as well as political. It will be seen later, upon studying the Prescript of the original Klan, that no such questions were asked of applicants for membership and no such restrictions imposed.

After the "alien" has satisfactorily answered the above ten questions, and has made his "donation," the first two sections of the obligation are administered, after which follow many papers of tiresome conversation.

After walking the candidate several times around the "Klavern," giving the various stationed officers the opportunity to spout forth "Simmonsese," the "alien" is led to the Exalted Cyclops who addresses a long "charge" to him, admonishing him of the great seriousness of the organization, and offering him an opportunity to retire and proceed no further. This offer is very largely a "bluff," because by this time the curiosity of the "alien" is at such a state that he would not think of retiring, and invariably he signifies that he desires to remain for the entire performance. There is more walking around, more verbose tommyrot, and

then the remainder of the oath is administered,
and the candidate is ready for "naturalization."

The "ceremony of naturalization" of the
"Invisible Empire" is a sacrilegious parody on
the holy rite of baptism, following a threat of
death if the "alien" violated his obligation to
"use any and all justifiable means and methods"
to carry out the work of the political machine!
There is no fraternal order in America which
has ever dared to do this, and I look back
upon the fact that I "baptized" a number of
men, who ought to have known better, with a
feeling of regret and humiliation.

After the "alien" has taken the entire obligation he is asked by the Exalted Cyclops:
"Sir, have you assumed without mental reservation your Oath of Allegiance to the 'Invisible
Empire' "? The "alien" answers in the affirma-
tive.

The Exalted Cyclops then warns him:
"Mortal man cannot assume a more binding
oath; character and courage alone will enable
you to keep it. Always remember that to
keep this oath means to you honor, happiness,
and life; but to violate it means disgrace,
dishonor and death. May happiness, honor and
life be yours."

Having been duly warned of death and dishonor, the "alien" is then led to the "sacred
altar" where rests the American flag, upon
which is the Holy Bible, opened at the twelfth
of Romans — which Simmons says is his

"spiritual charter"—and across the pages of
the Word of God is a naked dagger, grim
reminder of the preceding warning of the snake.
The Exalted Cyclops raises a glass of water,
and "dedicates" the "alien," setting him apart
from the men of his daily association to the
lofty service of the "Invisible Empire." He is
then caused to kneel upon his right knee, and
a parody on the beautiful hymn, "Just as I
am Without One Plea," is sung by those of the
elect who can carry a tune. Behind the "sacred
altar" burns the "fiery cross," which is an
upright piece of wood with a cross arm, in
which are set burning candles. When the singing is concluded, the Exalted Cyclops advances
to the candidate and after dedicating him
further, pours water on his shoulder, his head,
throws a few drops in the air, making his
dedication "in body," "in mind," "in spirit,"
and "in life." Having thus sacrilegiously
"baptized" the alien into the "Invisible Empire
of Ku Kluxism," the "Kludd," the chaplain of
the Klan — very often a minister of the gospel
— steps forward and delivers a prayer to God
to aid the candidate to keep his obligation, the
idea being, no doubt, that if God cannot or
will not prevent the "alien" from "keeping his
mouth shut," the dagger or the secret bullet of
the Ku Klux will!

The "alien" is then formally received as a
"citizen" of the "Invisible Empire," in the
name of the "Emperor," and is entitled to all

of the secret work of the organization, which is as tiresome and boring as the whole ritualistic twaddle. Most of this secret work is called the "Way of the Klavern," and is unimportant. One of the most interesting things of the "work" is the salute that each Klansman is required to give the American flag placed on a stand in the center of the room. The same salute is given whenever addressing the chair. It is the old salute of the Confederate Army, made with the right hand over the right eye, then reversing the hand so that the palm is in front.

The excessive number of signs and symbols used by the "Invisible Empire" are of no importance, but it will be of interest to mention the "Klonversation" which is a system of code words, by which one Ku Klux can know another. These code words are composed of the first letters of words in a sentence, and are used as a dialogue, as follows:

Upon meeting a stranger whom he wishes to test, the Klansman says:

AYAK, meaning, Are You A Klansman? the answer being, AKIA, A Klansman I Am.

CAPOWE, Countersign And Password Or Written Evidence?

CYGNAR, Can You Give Number And Realm?

No. 1, ATGA, Number One Klan of Atlanta, Ga.

KYGY, Klansman I Greet You.

ITSUB, In The Sacred Unfailing Bond,

(They shake hands with the left hand)

KLASP, Klannish Loyalty A Sacred Principle,

KABARK, Konstantly Applied By All Regular Klansmen.

The Exalted Cyclops then instructs the newly-made Klansman in the Countersign and Password, which at the present time are the words "White," and "Supremacy." The citizen is then solemnly instructed in the "MIOAK," or the Mystical Insignia of a Klansman, which is a cheap little celluloid button that is supposed to be the real innermost secret of Ku Kluxism. The MIOAK is red in color, and contains the letters KOTOP, with a square, and an extended open hand, and constitutes the emblem of the Klan. No explanation of the real meaning of the mystic words has ever been given, although the Kleagles generally tell their victims that it stands for "Knights of the Open Palm," a designation arising no doubt from the eagerness with which the open palm of the Kleagle is extended to receive the ten dollar "donations" so necessary in the manufacture of "citizens" from the "alien" raw material. The word Kotop is also used as a hailing word, its answer being "Potok," a reversal of the previous word. This is followed by the presentation of "Imperial Instructions," which is a booklet, "The Practice of Klanishness," containing many pages of the same wordy stuff with which the ritual is filled. This book enjoins the members to stick together in all things, but more especially to render at all times the greatest respect to the "Emperor" who is working day and night for the "cause," and for whom the "cause" is also working.

There is a long-winded, verbose and ridiculous "lecture" at the end of the "Kloran" that endeavors to give a history of the original Ku Klux Klan.

In the last two pages of the "Kloran" are to be found "titles and explanations" of the various officers and subdivisions of the "Invisible Empire," which have no importance to the general reader. It might be interesting, however, to note with what modesty "Emperor" Simmons speaks of himself when he writes:

"IMPERIAL WIZARD — The Emperor of the Invisible Empire; a wise man; a wonder-worker, having power to charm and control."

CHAPTER VIII

ANTI–NEGRO PROPAGANDA

I AM a white man.

I believe that the United States is a white man's country.

By all the instincts and traditions of my race, I believe that the United States having been created by white men will be ruled by white men. I do not believe that this doctrine applies merely to Tennessee and the rest of the Southern States, but to the entire country. In spite of innumerable criticisms hurled against the South in its handling of the negro, the entire country is gradually beginning to see that the South is right, because the South has demonstrated that the white race and the black race can live side by side and work side by side without friction. In cases where there is friction, the cause does not come from the best leadership of the South, as will be shown later on.

Experience has shown that the two races get along better when they are segregated. I expect to live to see the day when the people of the North provide separate schools for white and negro children, when negroes will not be elected to public office by white votes, and when politicians who cater to negro votes are sent to political oblivion. That such a condition will exist, I feel sure, but it will not be brought about by such organizations as the Knights of the Ku Klux Klan. It will come through an enlightenment of public opnion.

The activities of the Ku Klux Klan along the lines of race prejudice are the activities of the "professional Southerner," the political demagogue, and the sentiment of the "poor white" of the South. They are typical of the political spirit that has kept the South in bondage for thirty years, a spirit that has sent mediocre politicians to Congress and to other high offices, while abler men were shoved into the background.

The professional negro-baiter of the South has been greatly assisted by white people and negroes in the North, and I believe that the most valuable propaganda work for the Knights of the Ku Klux Klan which has been done along racial lines has been that of Senator Boies Penrose, of Pennsylvania. If Senator Penrose had been on the pay-roll of the Ku Klux Klan, and had been completely wrapped up in the success of the movement, he could not have secured more members than he did by issuing a statement to his negro constituents that the time had come to accord complete equality to the negro race. Of course Senator Penrose did not mean any such thing, but a public statement that he favored an equal rights' bill then pending at Harrisburg was a pleasant sop to the negro voters of Philadelphia who immediately saw visions of the dining room of the Bellevue-Stratford Hotel and the Adelphia. The fact that the members of the Pennsylvania legislature quickly and very quietly choked the bill to death showed the real sentiment of the white people of the State. The result in the South, however, was highly inflammatory. Carried by the Associated Press to every paper, its effect upon the minds of the people, especially the ignorant and uneducated, was like pouring gasoline on a hot stove. I am told that the enrollments of the Klan in the States comprising the "Black Belt" jumped by leaps and bounds, indicating that the ambitious Kleagles, looking for their four dollars a head, worked overtime in the use of the Penrose article.

Another piece of political clap-trap that aided the Ku Klux organizers was the action of the Speaker of the House, in the New Jersey legislature, in permitting a negro to occupy the speaker's chair during part of the last session. This was duly featured in the newspapers, and the Ku Klux Klan's workers very promptly asked the question: "Do you want this sort of thing to happen again in the South?" The answer came back most emphatically, "We do not." "Then give me your ten dollars and sign here," the organizer would reply. If there is a negro in the legislature of New Jersey, he was elected by white voters.

The periodical attempt of fanatical members of Congress to reduce the South's representation in that body on the ground that the negro is not permitted to vote have generally been featured in the newspapers, and much capital made of them by demagogic politicians. These things have aided the campaign of the Klan.

Another powerful recruiting force for the Ku Klux organization is the National Association for the Advancement of Colored Peoples, not "colored people" but "peoples," meaning no doubt people of all races except the white race. This organization through its press agency has issued statement after statement that has been eagerly taken up by the few papers that openly advocate Ku Kluxism, and used as effective propaganda in securing more members.

An examination of the list of field workers of the Knights of the Ku Klux Klan throughout the United States reveals the fact that strong propaganda work is being carried on in cities where there is a large negro population. In New York, Chicago, St. Louis, Cincinnati, Philadelphia, and Indianapolis are active and aggressive headquarters from which encouraging reports come to the Atlantic headquarters.

As a general proposition, I believe that the very existence of a secret organization bearing the name Ku Klux is having an effect of promoting unrest among the entire negro population of the South. While the negro cuts but little figure in the section in which I was working, I

learned from published reports and from conversations with newspaper men that there was
a feeling of great uneasiness among the Knoxville negroes due to the activities of the Klan.
In Chattanooga, where, on account of its anti-
Catholic propaganda, the Klan is making strong
headway, I found that the racial situation was
more accentuated. Chattanooga is a large and
important manufacturing center, and many
of the big plants employ negro labor. A negro
workman possessing the skill and ability requisite to hold his position can work at his trade in
Chattanooga, and as a general rule the laboring
classes of the negro race are industrious,
contented, prosperous and happy. In talking
with men closely identified with the manufacturing interests, I learned that the feeling of dis-
content and unrest is taking the place of the
negro's former attitude, and that should the Klan
succeed in gaining a substantial foothold it will
mean the emigration of large numbers of negro
laborers to Northern States, a thing that will
seriously cripple the industrial life of the city.
I found that the Chattanooga manufacturers,
almost to a man, were absolutely opposed to the
idea of having a Ku Klux Klan in the city.

All thinking men agree that the race question
in the United States is one of the most ominous
in the entire country. All right thinking people
desire it settled peacefully and in a way that will
not disturb the economic and industrial situation, I believe that, if left alone, the negro

will work out his own salvation. The history of the South for the past fifty years shows that the negro has been a most important factor in the development and upbuilding of the section.

My experience and observations on the race question has convinced me that in ninety-nine cases out of one hundred, where friction, serious or trivial, has occurred between the white and negro races, it has been due to the lower classes of the two races. Between the better-class white men and the better-class negro, there is, always has been, and always will be the best of feeling. I often have had Northern people say to me: "You Southern people hate negroes!" I always hasten to correct the statement, by replying, "The best people of the South not only do not hate a negro but they hold him in high esteem. The better class of Southern white man is the best friend the negro race has in this country today." The "hatred," if such is the word, exists between the low-class negro and the low-class white man, and if it were possible to analyze the real cause of the racial disorders in the country, it would probably be found that they are due to bad white men, bad negroes and bad whiskey.

While I make no charge that the Knights of the Ku Klux Klan have taken any part in them, it is a fact, nevertheless, that since this organization was started, there have been an abnormal number of instances of interracial friction. In the State of Georgia, where the Klan is probably strongest, there has been case after case of disorder. It seems to me that as an organization designed to aid the authorities in the enforcement of "law and order," the Ku Klux Klan has utterly failed to prevent these occurrences. If the Klan is capable of sustaining the arms of the law, why has it not done so in the State of Georgia?

Early in the summer of 1921, the whole country was shocked at the outbreak of a race riot in Tulsa, Okla., when an entire community was plunged into bloodshed and a vast amount of property destroyed. From the published accounts of the riot, it started from the most trivial cause imaginable, and in a short time white men and negroes were arrayed against each other in regular pitched battle. In examining the list of field workers of the Knights of the Ku Klux Klan, it is noticeable that there is a large force of Kleagles at work in the State of Oklahoma, and the presumption is that there is a Klan of Ku Kluxes in existence at Tulsa. Why did not the Klan rally to the support of the authorities and "enforce law and order?" The enforcement of law and order consists of stopping riot. Why was the riot not stopped? In this connection, I heard the leader of the Ku Klux Klan in Chattanooga, where I attended a large meeting shortly before resigning, make the statement that several weeks prior to the outbreak of the Tulsa riot he had been informed by a travelling man, also a Ku Klux, that a

clash between the races was likely to occur
within a short time. If this condition was a
true one, why were the authorities and their
valuable aids and abettors, the Ku Klux Klan,
not prepared to stop it?

A great bugaboo that is constantly harped
upon by the professional Southerner and by
the Ku Klux organizer is the cry of "social
equality" likely to be forced upon the white
people by the negro. This argument appeals
to the ignorant white man, but the intelligent
man knows that social equality between any
races or people is a myth. There is no such
thing as social equality between members of
the white race. Social equality is a matter of
opinion only, for while I might think that I
am superior to a person, that same person
might think that he is superior to me. Society
is split into strata made up largely through
community of interest, and congeniality of
ideas and thoughts. The man whose sole
thought in life is the accumulation of money
regards only his own kind as his equal; the
social butterfly skilled in the arts of polite
society looks with horror upon the "impossible" person who is not; the scholar seeks
solace and equality among people of brains;
and the philosopher, looking at the whole
human race with its follies and foibles, winks
at his brother philosopher and laughs at all
of them. When such a thing as social equality
exists between members of the white race,

then, and not until then, will it ever become
necessary seriously to consider the matter of
social equality between the white and black
races.

While I believe in the principles of a white
man's country and a white man's government,
I believe that the negro is as much entitled to
his life, liberty and the pursuit of happiness
as I am, and that he should be afforded all the
protection that the courts and laws of the
country can give him. I have seen cases tried
in the South where negroes have been convicted
of crime on evidence which, if presented against
a white man, would be thrown out of court.
Such cases are, however, uncommon, as I
believe the average officer of the law in the
South is usually fair and square in his treatment of the negro race.

The only way, in my judgment, that the
race question will ever be successfully handled
in the South, is by the promotion of better
feeling among the high-class men of both races,
and then have these men work on the lower
classes. Let the leaders of the negro race take
a strong stand in opposition to the vicious negro,
whose crimes against women and children have
done much toward placing the ban upon the
negro as a whole; and let the leaders of the
white race cast aside the demagogue and
impress upon the lower-class white man that
because his skin is white is no excuse for the
exercise of brutality toward the negro. Let

the proposition be sunk home that a white rough-neck, because his skin is white, has no warrant to ride roughshod over a decent and law-abiding negro because the latter's skin happens to be black.

In the Northern States, while the better class of negroes attend to their own business and conduct themselves well, the lower-class negro should be taught the value of decent behavior and good manners in public. Many negroes, particularly the vicious element, come to the North, and imagine that the treatment with which they are accorded gives them the license to crowd into the street cars, and make themselves offensive generally to white people. The negro with good manners wins his way wherever he goes, but the noisy, pugnacious individual, but newly arrived from the country of the "Jim Crow" street car does much to bring his entire race into disrepute. At the risk of arousing the ire of my Ku Klux friends, I advance the thought that a man can be a gentleman and a woman can be a lady even if their skins are black; and that people who are white can be offensive and boorish.

I am in favor of wiping out of our national life any organization, agency or association that tends to stir up the race question in any manner, shape or form, and leaving the subject to take care of itself under the guidance of men in the South who are devoting their lives to the work. In the city of Atlanta, there is an organization known as the Interracial Association headed by Rev. Ashby Jones, a Baptist minister, whose father, Rev. John William Jones was a chaplain in the Confederacy under General Lee. Men of the highest standing, including Dr. C. B. Wilmer, a well-known Episcopal minister of Atlanta, are in this movement, and I am informed that since they have commenced their activities, there has been a great deal of positive good accomplished in the elimination of discord between the white people and the negroes. On the other side, Doctor Moton, the head of the Tuskegee Institute, founded by Dr. Booker T. Washington, is going up and down the South, preaching sane things to the negro and to the white men. The leadership of these men represents the best thought and the best effort of both races in the South. The leadership of William J. Simmons and his Ku Klux Klan does not.

I think that the stirring up of the race question in the South, or elsewhere, for that matter, is at all times as dangerous as playing with dynamite, but the Ku Klux Klan has included in their propaganda against the negro its fight on the Catholics and Jews. While they do not specify in their ritual that this is the case, they imply it, and I have seen the actual propaganda as it is handled. The classification of the white Catholic and Jew with the negro is a stupid blunder, if nothing else. It is stupid, because, in the event of trouble on an extensive

scale stirred up by this organization or by its
psychological effect on the country, it is splitting
the white race into factions at a time when it
should stand together.

As I shall show further on, in discussing the
history and structure of the original Ku Klux
Klan, there is absolutely no racial condition
in the South or anywhere in America today that
warrants the existence of such an organization.
It is even worse than folly to make the religious
element figure into questions touching a section
where racial matters are always in the acute
stage.

In order to swell its roster, and to bring under
its banner of discord all the elements in the
country which it thinks it can handle, Ku
Kluxism is attempting to win the people of the
Pacific Coast by putting forth the doctrine of
"White Supremacy" in relation to the Japanese
question. I have seen and heard read many
reports from California indicating that the
Kleagles on the coast are doing a land office
business and that the people are "donating ten
dollars" to the "noble cause" as rapidly as
they can sign the petition for citizenship.
Without regard to the merits or demerits of
the Japanese question, as it affects the people
of California, there again creeps into the subject
the discrimination against white men by class-
ing them as foreigners along with the Japanese.
I know nothing of the industrial conditions of
California, but I am quite sure that a portion of

the prosperity and greatness of the State has been developed by Catholic and Jewish people.

As a general proposition Southern people are exceptionally capable of sympathizing with Californians in their peculiar racial problem, and would probably back them in every way that is legitimate, but the Japanese question is an international one, and should be and must be handled by the State department in Washington, and not by the "Emperor" of the "Invisible Empire" in Atlanta. The carrying on of a vigorous campaign for members of the Ku Klux Klan on the Pacific Coast is an infringement on the duties and prerogatives of the United States Government. If it is not stopped, it is likely to lead to unpleasant and dangerous international consequences.

CHAPTER IX

RELIGIOUS PROPAGANDA

ONE of the strongest pieces of evidence that the Simmons monstrosity is not "the genuine original Klan," and that its claim to being "a monument to the Confederate soldier" is an insult to the cause headed by Jefferson Davis and Robert E. Lee, is its propaganda of religious animosity and prejudice, which is directed specifically at Catholics and Jews. While it claims to be a great and "noble cause" for the "uplift" of humanity, the protection of womanhood, the enforcement of law and order and the maintenance of "white supremacy," I am firmly convinced that its fundamental idea is the creation of a secret political Empire for the purpose of totally eliminating Catholics and Jews from public life.

It is a rather surprising thing to me that a man who claims to have spent a part of his life as a professor of history in any college should be so strangely unfamiliar with the composition of the Southern Confederacy. I wonder if Simmons ever heard of Judah P. Benjamin! One of the foremost and ablest men in the cabinet of Mr. Davis was a Jew! I wonder if the Imperial Wizard and Emperor of the

Invisible Empire ever looked into the military records of the Confederate Army and saw the large number of Jewish names, and if he knows that among some of the best and bravest soldiers the South ever had the Jew was very much in evidence. I wonder if Simmons ever heard of Pat Clebourne, the fighting Irishman who gave a good account of himself every time he went into action, or if he ever read the beautiful poems of Father Ryan, a Catholic priest who followed the Stars and Bars into the very jaws of hell to comfort the wounded and administer to the dying. There was scarcely a company of infantry a troop of cavalry or battery of artillery, that did not have an Irish Catholic on its roster, and they soldiered and suffered and fought and died for the South along with their Protestant comrades. Yet, in the year 1915, is commenced the erection of a "monument to the Confederate soldier" in the shape of a secret, Jew-baiting, Catholic-baiting, Negro-hating, money-getting proposition that has the effrontery to call itself the name of the "Ku Klux Klan," and to presume with its white-robed and masked members, to interfere with the administration of justice in the United States.

Along the lines of anti-Catholicism, the organization is working hard. Among the very first consignments of printed matter I received from "The Gate City Manufacturing Company" of Atlanta was a lot of cards, bearing no imprint, but asking several questions about the Catholic Church. The following is a copy:

"DO YOU KNOW?"

"That the pope is a political autocrat.

"That a secret treaty made by him started the war.

"That he is enthroned and crowned and makes treaties and sends and receives ambassadors.

"That one hundred and sixteen princes of his government are enthroned in our cities.

"That he has courts here enforcing the canon law.

"That he controls the daily and magazine press.

"That he denounces popular government as inherently vicious.

"That his canon law condemns public schools and forbids children to attend them.

"That popery enthroned in great cities controls politics.

"That our war industries were placed exclusively in Roman Catholic hands.

"That no sectarian body or fraternal order but Knights of Columbus was permitted to do war-relief work in the army and navy.

"That Roman Catholics compose one-sixth of our population and hold three-fourths of the public offices, being entrenched in national, state, and city governments throughout the country.

"That they are pouring into our land as immigrants at the rate of two millions a year.

"That Knights of Columbus declare they will make popery dominant in the United States.

"Let us arouse the people and save our country as the beacon light of constitutional liberty and the hope of the world."

Among the methods used by propagandists of the Ku Klux Klan in enlisting recruits by means of attacks on the Catholic Church is a certain bogus oath purporting to be the obligation assumed by members of the Fourth Degree of the Knights of Columbus. This oath first made its appearance in this country in 1912, and was widely circulated by anti-Catholics. In 1913, in a contested election case involving a seat in Congress from Pennsylvania, Eugene C. Bonniwell, himself a Catholic, filed charges with a Congressional Committee that this alleged oath had been circulated by his opponent Thomas S. Butler, who denied that he had been responsible for such circulation and had urged his followers that they refrain from circulating the oath. Purely as a matter of a legal exhibit, a copy of this "oath" was ordered printed in the Congressional Record, February 15, 1913. The document as given in the Congressional Record reads as follows:

"KNIGHTS OF COLUMBUS OATH.   FOURTH DEGREE

"I, — —— ——, now in the presence of Almighty God, the blessed Virgin Mary, the blessed St. John the Baptist, the Holy Apostles, St. Peter and St. Paul, and all the saints, sacred host of Heaven, and to you, my Ghostly Father, the superior general of the Society of Jesus, founded by St. Ignatius Loyola, in the pontification of Paul the III, and continued to the present, do by the womb of the Virgin, the matrix of God, and the rod of Jesus Christ, declare and swear that His Holiness, the Pope, is Christ's vice-regent and is the true and only head of the Catholic or Universal Church throughout the earth; and that by virtue of the keys of binding and loosing given his Holiness by my Saviour, Jesus Christ, he hath power to depose heretical kings, princes, States, Commonwealths, and Governments and they may be safely destroyed. Therefore to the utmost of my power, I will defend this doctrine and His Holiness's right and custom against all usurpers of the heretical or Protestant authority whatever, especially the Lutheran Church of Germany, Holland, Denmark, Sweden, and Norway, and the now pretended authority and Churches of England and Scotland, and the branches of same now established in Ireland, and on the Continent of America and elsewhere, and all adherents in regard that they may be usurped and heretical opposing the sacred Mother Church of Rome.

"I do now denounce and disown any allegiance as due to any heretical king, prince, or State, named Protestant or Liberals, or obedience to any of their laws, magistrates, or officers.

"I do further declare that the doctrine of the Churches of England and Scotland, of the Calvinists, Huguenots, and others of the name of Protestants or Masons to be damnable, and they themselves to be damned who will not forsake the same.

"I do further declare that I will help, assist, and advise all or any of His Holiness's agents, in any place where I should be, in Switzerland, Germany, Holland, Ireland, or America, or in any other kingdom or territory I shall come to, and do my utmost to extirpate the heretical Protestant or Masonic doctrines and to destroy all their pretended powers, legal or otherwise.

"I do further promise and declare that, notwithstanding that I am dispensed with to assume any religion heretical for the propaganda of the Mother Church's interest, to keep secret and private all her agents' counsels from time to time, as they instruct me, and not divulge, directly or indirectly, by word, writing, or circumstances whatever, but to execute all that should be proposed, given in charge, or discovered unto me by you, my Ghostly Father, or any of this sacred order.

"I do further promise and declare that I will have no opinion or will of my own or any mental reservation whatsoever, even as a corpse or cadaver (perinde ac cadaver), but will unhesitatingly obey each and every command that I may receive from my superiors in the militia of the Pope and of Jesus Christ.

"That I will go to any part of the world whithersoever I may be sent, to the frozen regions North, jungles of India, to the centers of civilization of Europe, or to the wild haunts of the barbarous savages of America without murmuring or repining, and will be submissive in all things whatsoever is communicated to me.

"I do further promise and declare that I will, when opportunity presents, make and wage relentless war, secretly and openly, against all heretics, Protestants and Masons, as I am directed to do, to extirpate them from the face of the whole earth; and that I will spare neither age, sex or condition, and that I will hang, burn, waste, boil, flay, strangle, and bury alive these infamous heretics; rip up the stomachs and wombs of their women, and crash their infants' heads against the walls in order to annihilate their execrable race. That when the same can not be done openly, I will secretly use the poisonous cup, the strangulation cord, the steel of the poniard, or the leaden bullet, regardless of the honor, rank, dignity, or authority of the persons, whatever may be their condition in life, either public or private, as I at any time may be directed so to do by any agents of the Pope or superior of the Brotherhood of the Holy Father of the Society of Jesus.

"In confirmation of which I hereby dedicate my life, soul, and all corporal powers, and with the dagger which I now receive I will subscribe my name written in my blood in testimony thereof; and should I prove false or weaken in my determination, may my brethren and fellow soldiers of the militia of the Pope cut off my hands and feet and my throat from ear to ear, my belly opened and sulphur burned therein with all the punishment that can be inflicted upon me on earth and my soul shall be tortured by demons in eternal hell forever.

"That I will in voting always vote for a K. of C. in

preference to a Protestant especially a Mason, and that I will leave my party so to do; that if two Catholics are on the ticket I will satisfy myself which is the better supporter of Mother Church and vote accordingly.

"That I will not deal with or employ a Protestant if in my power to deal with or employ a Catholic. That I will place Catholic girls in Protestant families that a weekly report may be made of the inner movements of the heretics.

"That I will provide myself with arms and ammunition that I may be in readiness when the word is passed, or I am commanded to defend the church, either as an individual or with the militia of the Pope.

"All of which, I, ———— ————, do swear by the blessed Trinity and blessed sacrament which I am now to receive to perform and on part to keep this, my oath.

"In testimony hereof, take this most holy and blessed Sacrament of the Eucharest and witness the same further with my name written with the point of this dagger dipped in my own blood and seal in the face of this holy sacrament." (Excerpts from "Contested election case of Eugene C. Bonniwell against Thos. S. Butler," as appears in the Congressional Record —— house, Feb. 15, 1913, at pages 3215, etc., and ordered printed therein "by unanimous consent." Attached thereto and printed (on page 3216) as a part of said report as above.)"

While I was engaged in the work as Kleagle of the "Invisible Empire," I was given copies of this "oath" by four travelling men who had previously identified themselves to me as Klansmen, and was informed that it had been and was being widely circulated, not only in their home towns, but all through the South by workers in the Ku Klux cause. I had not previously seen this oath, and without investigating its authenticity permitted it to be

reprinted and circulated in my territory,
although the men who became members of the
Klan under me did not attach any genuineness
to the document. There was, therefore, but
comparatively little use made of it in my territory, but I learned that in Knoxville and
Chattanooga it was freely and industriously
circulated. Among the ignorant classes of
people, I learned, the oath was accepted as
genuine, and was the means of securing a large
number of members for Ku Kluxism. In
Chattanooga, in May, 1921, the convention of
the Southern Baptists was held, and as a great
many speeches were made against Romanism,
the public mind was in a very responsive mood
to accept the alleged oath as the real obligation
of the Knights of Columbus. I made inquiry
of my King Kleagle as to whether or not the
Atlanta people were printing and distributing the
"oath."

In a letter written to me from Chattanooga,
dated May 25, 1921, the King Kleagle, said:

"The Imperial Palace does not get out copies of the
K. C. oath but I find it of value among a certain few.

"I find papers like the *Protestant* that I suggested
your subscribing for to be the most valuable dope that
I can use for it brings home in a concrete form to them
the things we have to guard against."

Having been, in a limited way, a party to the
distribution of this oath, I feel that it is my
duty to print the result of my investigations
as to its nature and also to give in full the

real obligation of the Fourth Degree Knights
of 'Columbus which was made public in the
summer of 1921. It appears from my investigations that several times the authenticity of the
"oath" has been brought into the courts by
the Knights of Columbus, and each time it has
been proven to be a fraud. An instance occurred,
however, that is so strongly convincing that
every American who believes in fair play,
especially every Mason in the country, should
know about it. In Los Angeles, California, in
1914, the State Deputy of the Knights of
Columbus submitted the entire work, ceremonies
and pledges of his order to a committee of
Masons made up of Messrs. Motley Hewes
Flint, thirty-third degree, Past Grand Master
of California, Dana Reid Weller, Past Grand
Master, William Rhodes Hewey, Past Master,
and Samuel E. Burke, Inspector of the Los
Angeles Masonic District. These gentlemen
made a careful examination of the entire subject, and rendered the following report:

"We hereby certify that by authority of the highest
officer of the Knights of Columbus in the State of California, who acted under instructions from the Supreme
Officer of the Order in the United States, we were furnished a complete copy of all the work, ceremonies and
pledges used by the Order, and that we carefully read,
discussed and examined the same. We found that while
in a sense the Order is a secret association, it is not an oath-
bound organization and that its ceremonies are comprised
in four degrees, which are intended to teach and inculcate
principles that lie at the foundation of every great religion

and every free state. Our examination of these ceremonials
and obligations was made primarily for the purpose of
ascertaining whether or not a certain alleged oath of the
Knights of Columbus, which has been printed and widely
circulated, was in fact used by the Order and whether
if it was not used, any oath, obligation or pledge was
used which was or would be offensive to Protestants or
Masons, or those who are engaged in circulating a document of peculiar viciousness and wickedness. We find
that neither the alleged oath nor any oath or pledge
bearing the remotest resemblance thereto in matter,
manner, spirit or purpose is used or forms a part of the
ceremonies of any degree of the Knights of Columbus.
The alleged oath is scurrilous, wicked and libelous and
must be the invention of an impious and venomous mind.
We find that the Order of Knights of Columbus, as shown
by its rituals, is dedicated to the Catholic religion, charity
and patriotism. There is no propaganda proposed or
taught against Protestants or Masons or persons not of
Catholic faith. Indeed, Protestants and Masons are not
referred to directly or indirectly in the ceremonials and
pledges. The ceremonial of the Order teaches a high
and noble patriotism, instills a love of country, inculcates
a reverence for law and order, urges the conscientious and
unselfish performance of civic duty, and holds up the
Constitution of our country as the richest and most
precious possession of a Knight of the Order. We can
find nothing in the entire ceremonial of the Order that
to our minds could be objected to by any person."

The real oath or pledge of the Fourth
Degree of the Knights of Columbus reads:

"I swear to support the Constitution of the United
States. I pledge myself as a Catholic citizen and Knight
of Columbus, to enlighten myself fully upon my duties as
a citizen and to conscientiously perform such duties
entirely in the interest of my country and regardless of all
personal consequences. I pledge myself to do all in my

power to preserve the integrity and purity of the ballot, and to promote reverence and respect for law and order. I promise to practice my religion openly and consistently but without ostentation, and to so conduct myself in public affairs, and in the exercise of public virtue as to reflect nothing but credit upon our Holy Church, to the end that she may flourish and our country prosper to the greater honor and Glory of God."

When one pauses to examine into the history of the old Ku Klux Klan, and the objects for which it was organized, it seems almost incredible that any organization claiming to be the "genuine original Klan" would stoop to belittle the memory of the old Klan by making capital of religious prejudice. As will be shown further along in my narrative, there were absolutely no restrictions in the old Klan as to religious belief, the Precept clearly setting forth the qualifications for membership. Nothing whatever was said about a Jew, a Catholic or a person who happened to be born in a foreign country. While I was working in Johnson City, I took into the organization an old gentleman who had been a member of the original Klan at Morristown. There is a rule that "original Klansmen" are not required to make any "donations" or pay any dues. When this old ex-Confederate soldier was taken in, it was at the end of my career as Kleagle, and as I swore him to the un-American obligation, I could not help feeling ashamed and disgusted. I had several conversations with him afterwards, and asked him specifically as to the regulations of

the old Klan in reference to members. He stated
positively that there were no rules whatever
prohibiting Catholics and Jews from becoming
Klansmen, and that one of the best men in his
Den was a German who had been born in
in Germany. On account of the fact that
he had associated intimately with Jewish and
Catholic Confederate soldiers, the old gentleman expressed himself as being amazed that,
in an attempt to revive the Klan, any such discrimination should be practiced.

I received a number of copies of the *Protestant*, for which the King Kleagle McArthur,
advised me to subscribe because, he wrote,
"It brings home in concrete form to them
the things we have to guard against." This
paper is published in Washington, D. C., and is
of the usual type of rabidly anti-Catholic
publication. An examination of some of its
headlines shows the character of its attacks.
This paper was eagerly read by Ku Kluxes
wherever it circulated and was indeed a valuable
agency in securing recruits.

I also heard other Kleagles attack Catholicism,
most of the attacks appealing to me as being
ridiculous, one especially which stated that the
Catholic Church was financially backing the
National Association for the Advancement of
Colored Peoples. It was gravely stated that the
Catholics were arming the negroes of the South
and that at the "right time" would join in an
armed uprising to seize the country.

Considerable anti-Catholic propaganda has been and is being published in the columns of the *Searchlight* the official organ of the Ku Klux Klan. Among the statements I have seen was an intimation that the Catholic Church was responsible for the murder of President Abraham Lincoln. Copies of the *Searchlight* are sent to each Kleagle for distribution among his Klans, and I received a number of copies in my connection with the organization. In every town there is a Klansman, either paid for his services or who renders same gratuitously, who makes a speciality of getting subscribers for the *Searchlight* and of placing the publication on the news stands.

In the issue of August 6, 1921, the *Searchlight* printed on its first page an article by Rev. Caleb A. Ridley, a Baptist preacher of Atlanta, part of which stated:

"Some people seem to think that the Ku Klux Klan is a body of men who have banded together simply to oppose certain things they do not like — that they are anti-Jew, anti-Catholic, anti-negro, anti-foreign, anti-everything. But real Klansmen have no fight to make on any of these. I can't help being what I am racially. I am not a Jew, nor a negro, nor a foreigner. I am an Anglo-Saxon white man, so ordained by the hand and will of God, and so constituted and trained that I cannot conscientiously take either my politics or religion from some secluded ass on the other side of the world.

"Now, if somebody else is a Jew, I can't help it any more than he can. Or, if he happens to be black, I can't help that either. If he were born under some foreign flag, I couldn't help it, and if he wants to go clear back to

Italy for his religion and his politics, I cannot hinder
him; but there is one thing I can do. I can object to his
un-American propaganda being preached in my home or
practiced in the solemn assembly of real Americans."

The propaganda against the Jew is being
carried on as viciously as against the Catholic.
In the *Searchlight* of July 30, 1921, there
appeared on the front page a typical anti-Semitic
article in the nature of a letter written from
New York, and signed "American," of which
the following is an extract:

"The Jew is interested in creating war between blacks
and whites, not to benefit the negro, but to destroy our
government. For the same reason, the Jew is interested
in overthrowing Christian Russia. But remember, he
does not intend to stop at Russia. Through his Third
Internationale of Moscow he is working to overthrow
all the Gentile governments of the world. I am enclosing
an editorial clipped from the *New York World* of Saturday,
July 23. You will keep in mind that the *World* is Jew-
owned (as is also every newspaper in New York City
except the *Tribune*).

"My investigation proved to me beyond a doubt that
the negro situation is being made increasingly dangerous
by Jewish agitators.

"In all my twenty-five years travelling over this continent, I have never met a disloyal American who failed
to be either foreign born or a Semite.

"With the best wishes for the success of the Ku Klux
Klan."

CHAPTER X

The Original Ku Klux Klan

The destiny of the United States, like the destiny of the individual, lies not in dwelling upon the unpleasant things of the past but in a sane and correct solution of the problems of the present and of the future. We are all Americans; we live amid conditions that demand national unity and national sanity; and our principal thought should be the elimination of sectional discord and internal dissension. Experience has shown me that there is but little basic difference between average Americans, no matter in what part of the country they may have been born and reared. Aside from local customs, variations of accent, and minor provincialisms, the man from Tennessee is no different from the man from Massachusetts, and the man from New Jersey is a brother "under his skin" to the "native son" of the Golden West. To remove the causes of friction, to eliminate sectional and class hatred, and to inculcate the principles of unified Americanism among people of diversified interests are the real ideals of this Republic.

Believing, therefore, that constant dwelling upon the evil of the past is unhealthful, both to the individual and to the nation, it is neither my intention nor purpose, in discussing the historical side of the original Ku Klux Klan to give vent to the passions and prejudices of the South of the days immediately following the Civil War. In dealing with it, I am merely narrating facts as set forth by men recognized as authorities of American history, and these facts can, if need be, be verified by the reader.

It is a part of the tragedy of war that its termination is followed by a period of painful reconstruction. Every war ever fought in the world's history has had its inevitable aftermath of readjustment — the return from the abnormal to the normal. In some instances this has been so imperceptible as to entail but little hardship upon the people who have suffered the terrible effects of armed conflict; in others, the harshness of the conqueror to the conquered and the brutality of the victor toward the vanquished have left traces of hatred and lust for vengeance that have survived for generations.

In the study of the history of the Anglo-Saxon race, there are two reconstruction periods that stand out in marked contrast. One was the reconstruction of the Southern States following the Civil War, and the other was the reconstruction of South Africa by the British government immediately after the Boer War. The former was handled in a stupid, ignorant, and insane manner, and based upon the lust of spoils and upon the most wretched of partisan politics.

The latter was disposed of in a wise, sane, and statesmanly fashion, with impartial consideration for the welfare of the British Empire and the peace and good will of the Boers.

The reconstruction of the Southern States following the Civil War was utterly stupid, and Americans of our generation — regardless of Northern or Southern birth — so consider it, and know that the manner in which the situation was handled was a political mistake.

The activities of the "carpetbaggers" and their negro allies after the Civil War were not confined merely to the looting of the public treasuries. Vicious white men organized the negroes into societies and stirred up their hatred against the white people, with the result that unspeakable crimes were committed in all parts of the South. Perhaps the most notorious of these organizations was that known as the "Loyal League," which operated in all parts of the South, and which was composed of negroes and low white men.

I quote from Mr. Wilson's work, the following clear and well-worded summary:

"The price of the policy to which it gave the final touch of permanence was the temporary disintegration of Southern society and the utter, apparently the irretrievable alienation of the South from the political party whose mastery it had been Mr. Stevens' chief aim to perpetuate. The white men of the South were aroused by the mere instinct of self-preservation to rid themselves, by fair means or foul, of the intolerable burden of governments sustained by the votes of ignorant negroes and conducted in the interest of adventurers: governments whose incredible debts were incurred that thieves might be enriched, whose increasing loans and taxes went to no public use but into the pockets of party managers and corrupt contractors. There was no place of open action or of constitutional agitation, under the terms of reconstruction, for the men who were the real leaders of the Southern communities. The restrictions shut white men of the older order out from the suffrage even. They could act only by private combination, by private means, as a force outside the government, hostile to it, prescribed by it, of whom opposition and bitter resistance was expected, and expected with defiance. . . . But there were men to whom counsels of prudence seemed as ineffectual as they were unpalatable, men who could not sit still and suffer what was now put upon them. . . . They took the law into their own hands and began to attempt by intimidation what they were not allowed to attempt by the ballot or by any course of public action."

The agency by which the South was saved from the devilish scheme of Thaddeus Stevens to Africanize it and convert it into a mongrel, half-bred section was the original Ku Klux Klan! Brought into being by chance, and used as an agency to meet the exigency of the hour, it served its purpose as many similar systems have served theirs, including the Western vigilantes, whose work has been commended by Theodore Roosevelt on the ground of public necessity. Then having restored the South to the control of its better element, it passed away, to occupy a cherished place in the history of the Southern States, from which it can never be resurrected.

The reign of Ku Kluxism existed in the
Southern States from the year 1866 until
President Rutherford B. Hayes withdrew the
Federal troops from the South, during which
period a number of its phases present themselves for study and investigation. In some of
these, if one accepts the opinions of radical
members of Congress from the Northern States,
the whole system was nothing but evil; while
if the extremely radical Southern viewpoint
is accepted, the Ku Klux movement was as
spotless as a lily and was responsible for no
acts of lawlessness whatever. Somewhere
between the extreme Northern condemnation
and the extreme Southern justification lies the
truth. In any case the Ku Klux movement
was the exercise of extra-legal force for the
purpose of meeting a revolutionary condition
of society in a revolutionary manner. In the
sense that it had no standing in law and took
upon itself to enforce what its leaders saw fit
to declare was the law, it was an outlaw organization. Taken by itself, in the light of our
present system of government and law enforcement, it has nothing on which to stand; but,
studied in the light of the reconstruction period,
it is shown to have been the last desperate resort
of the Anglo-Saxon to resist and overthrow
the attempt to Afracanize his country.

The movement was a revolution to meet a
situation unparalled in this country's history,
and the history of revolutions has never at any

time manifested the character of pink teas or church socials. Personally I prefer to adopt the point of view that in a chaotic and despotic condition of society like the one forced upon the Southern people, the end justified the means, and would place the entire responsibility of what happened in the South upon the shoulders of Thaddeus Stevens and other radical leaders of Congress.

A careful investigation of the history of the original movement shows that it was divided into three separate and distinct periods. It was first organized as a secret society for the amusement of its members, without any serious attempt to act as a "regulator" of social and political affairs; it was then transformed into a great political-military movement, enforced law and order, drove the negro and the carpetbagger out of politics, and was then ordered disbanded; and lastly it attempted in unorganized fashion, without the authority of its former leaders, to rule many communities, and an enormous number of acts of violence were committed either by it or in its name.

There were several different organizations which sprang into existence in the South during the reconstruction periods, each one operating along the same general lines but bearing different names. There were the Ku Klux Klan, the White Brotherhood, the Pale Faces, the Constitutional Union Guards, and the Knights of the White Camelia, which was larger than any of them. In the latter days of the reconstruction, when acts of lawlessness in the South were so bad that an investigation was held by Congress, the general name of Ku Klux was applied to all extra-legal Southern movements. As this narrative deals only with the Ku Klux Klan, a discussion of the other movements is unnecessary.

The Ku Klux Klan was organized in Pulaski, Tenn., in May, 1866. Several young men who had served in the Confederate Army, having returned to their homes, found themselves suffering from the inactivity and reaction that followed army life. There was nothing to do in which to relieve it. There was but little work to do, and but few had capital to engage in new mercantile or professional pursuits. The amusements and diversions of normal society were lacking, and to meet this situation, it was decided to form a secret society merely for the purpose of burlesque and fun-making. After the society was organized, and a name was sought, one of the members suggested the word "*kukloi*" from the Greek word "*Kuklos*" meaning circle. Another member then suggested: "Call it 'Ku Klux,' " and this suggestion was at once adopted, with the addition of the word Klan.

The new society was a success from the start. The "joiner" of 1866 was no different from the "joiner" of 1921. The boys made the organization one of deep mystery; they adopted

grotesque and hideous costumes which they
wore to and from their places of initiation;
they gave out hints of the wonders of the new
society, which played on the curiosity of the
public; and they had mysterious communications printed in the local newspapers. The
members were required to maintain profound
and absolute secrecy with reference to everything connected with the order, and went at
their work with great glee, to the added mystifi-
cation of the community. The result was that
everybody in the city of Pulaski and all throughout the surrounding country, became possessed
of the "joiner's itch" and sought admission.
No applications were solicited for membership,
because the organizers knew human nature
well enough to know that if they gave out the
impression that they wished to be exclusive the
applications would be both voluntary and
numerous. The organization grew very rapidly,
and strangers coming to Tennessee from other
Southern States learned of it, became members,
and secured permission to start local organizations. By the fall and winter of 1866 the order
had grown all over the South, and in nearly
every community there was a "Den" of Ku
Kluxes enjoying the baffled curiosity and wild
speculations of a mystified public.

In March, 1867, the Reconstruction Acts were
passed by Congress, and in the month of April
the actual work of reconstruction began. Then
it was that the Ku Klux Klan underwent its

second stage of development and became transformed into a band of regulators to handle the alarming situation that immediately followed. Perhaps the best available authority on the Klan in the country today is a little book written by Capt. John C. Lester and Rev. D. L. Wilson, giving an insight into its organization and real history. Captain Lester was one of the six original organizers, and Mr. Wilson, while not a member, was a resident of Pulaski and was closely in touch with the entire movement. In this work they stated that the transformation of the society was effected in three ways:

(1) The impressions made by the order upon those who joined it; (2) the impressions made upon the public by it; (3) the anomalous and peculiar condition of affairs in the South at the time. The impression made upon the man who joined was that behind all the amusement features of the organization and, unexpressed in its ritualistic work, was a deep purpose — a solemn mission that would be undertaken later. What it was none knew, but the feeling existed that a mission existed, just the same. The impressions made upon the public immediately showed the Klansmen that the organization possessed a certain power that nobody had imagined it would possess. This power was largely one of fright and intimidation, and was shown in the case of the ignorant and superstitious negro more than in that of the white

people. Negroes would see the ghostly nocturnal
Ku Kluxes and imagine that they were spirits
of deceased Confederate soldiers, and the Klansmen were very quick to grasp the idea and use
it to the fullest advantage. In some cases a
figure in white would ride up to a negro's house,
dismount and ask for a drink of water. The
frightened negro would hand him a gourd,
which the rider would pour into a rubber bag,
concealed under his robe, and then demand a
whole bucketful of water, which he would dispose
of in the same way, remarking, "That was the
first drink of water I have had since I was killed
at Shiloh." In other cases the Ku Klux members
would wear false heads, ride up to a negro and,
removing the head, ask the negro to hold it.
Skeleton hands would be fastened to the wrist
and held out for a handshake, which procedure
usually caused the terrified negro to make a
hasty retreat. With the superstition and natural
tendency of their race to magnify happenings,
the negroes soon spread alarming tales among
themselves as to the Ku Klux and its doings,
until presently the name was one that invoked
horror and terror. It is but natural, therefore,
that knowing this new power of frightening the
negro, the members of the strange order exercised
it to the fullest extent.

In May, 1867, in order to form a strong sectional organization, a convention was secretly
held at Nashville, Tenn., and the Prescript of
the order was revised and amended by dele-

gates from all of the States. Plans were made
for extensive work, and for propagating the
order in every community in the South. Gen.
Nathan B. Forrest, having previously heard
of the organization made a careful investigation
of it, and consented to become its head, assuming
the office of Grand Wizard immediately after the
Nashville Convention. He had been one of the
South's most successful and distinguished
cavalry officers, was recognized as being able
to handle men in a masterful manner, and was
a person of coolness and clear-headed judgment.
He at once set to work to reorganize the order,
which had become more or less demoralized
under loose management, and made it a real
factor in handling the serious situation which
grew more serious as the reconstruction proceeded. He brought the membership in Tennessee up to 40,000 and the total membership
in the South to 550,000, and did all he could
to keep the force in strong control.

A great many of the most prominent men
in the South became members of the organization, and were either active in the work or
served in an advisory capacity. Among them
were Generals John B. Gordon, A. H. Colquitt,
G. T. Anderson and A. R. Lawton, of Georgia,
Gen. W. J. Hardee, Gen. John C. Brown, Capt.
John W. Morton, Gen. George W. Gordon, and
Gen. Albert Pike, who later became one of the
foremost Masonic authorities in the country. Gen.
Pike was the chief judicial officer of the Klan.

Among the first policies inaugurated by General Forrest was the courting of widespread publicity, and an order was issued for a parade in full regalia on July 4, 1867. In every Southern city parades of the Ku Klux Klans were held, and served to act as an advertisement to the people of the South that they were being protected, and to serve notice on the carpetbagger and the negro that a new force had arisen for the purpose of meeting their encroachments upon the liberties of the white people.

Then began the reign of the mysterious organization that ended in the various restorations of the State government to the white people of the South, most of which occurred in 1870, the last States to throw off the yoke being South Carolina and Louisiana. What occurred during that time in the way of actual events is but vaguely stated.

The fact that the whole period was one of the bitterest of partisan politics makes it necessary to discount to a large degree the statements of both sides of the controversy. It has been told by some that the original Ku Klux Klan enforced its decrees and maintained law and order, not so much by the overt acts it committed but by reason of the vague fear and surmises on the part of the negro and carpetbagger as to what the Klan could do.

In an address before the Bar Association of Texas in 1906, Hon. Thomas W. Gregory, later Attorney-General of the United States, gave a history of the old Klan, and in speaking of its work said:

"It is safe to say that ninety per cent of the work of the Klan involved no act of personal violence. In most instances mere knowledge of the fact that the Ku Klux were organized in the community and patrolled it by night accomplished most that was desired. In the case of nocturnal meetings of the negroes, organized by scalawags and carpetbaggers, which proved disorderly and offensive, sheeted horsemen would be found drawn up across every road leading from the meeting place; and although not a word was spoken and no violence whatever offered, that meeting was usually adjourned *sine die.* . . . But masked riders and mystery were not the only Ku Klux devices. Carpetbaggers and scalawags and their families were ostracized in all walks of life — in the church, in the school, in business, wherever men and women or even children gathered together, no matter what the purpose or the place, the alien and the renegade, and all that belonged or pertained to them were refused recognition and consigned to outer darkness and the companionship of negroes.

"In addition to these methods, there were some of a much more drastic nature. The sheeted horseman did not merely warn and intimidate, especially when the warnings were not heeded. In many instances negroes and carpetbaggers were whipped and in rare instances shot or hanged. Notice to leave the country was frequently extended and rarely declined, and if declined the results were likely to be serious. Hanging was promptly administered to the house burner and sometimes to the murderer; the defamer of women of good character was usually whipped and sometimes executed if the offense was repeated; threats of violence and oppression of the weak and defenseless if persisted in after due warning met with drastic and sometimes cruel remedies; mere corruption in public office was too universal for punishment or even comment, but he who prostituted official power to oppress the individual, a crime prevalent from one end of the country to the other, especially in cases where it affected the widow and orphan, was likely to be dealt with in no gentle way, in case a warning was not promptly observed; those who advocated and practiced social equality of the races and incited hostility of the blacks against the whites were given a single notice to depart in haste, and they rarely took time to reply."

Whether one looks upon the methods of the Ku Klux Klan as wise and humane or as rough and cruel, the fact remains that its work was accomplished, and state governments under carpetbag control, negro militia, acts of Congress and proclamations of the President though backed by the army of the United States, made but little headway against the silent force of white men which was making a last desperate stand for all they held sacred.

Lester and Wilson in commenting on the work of the Klan, even before it was transformed into a movement of regulators say:

"The order contained within itself, by reason of the methods practiced, sources of weakness. The devices and disguises by which the Klan deceived outsiders enabled all who were so disposed, to practice deception on the Klan itself. It placed in the hands of its own members the facility to do deeds of violence for the gratification of personal feeling, and have them credited to the Klan. To evilly disposed men membership in the Klan was an inducement to wrongdoing. It presented to all men a dangerous temptation, which, in certain contingencies at any time likely to arise, it required a considerable amount of moral robustness to resist. Many did not withstand it. Up to this time, the majority had shown a fair appreciation of the responsibilities of their self-imposed task of preserving social order. But under any circumstances the natural tendency of an organization such as this is to violence and crime — much more under such circumstances as those then prevailing."

In September, 1868, Governor Brownlow of Tennessee called the legislature into session, and caused a drastic act to be passed comparable only to the Reconstruction Acts of Congress. Under its terms association or connection with the Ku Klux Klan was punishable by a fine of $500 and imprisonment in the penitentiary for not less than five years. Any inhabitant of the State was constituted an officer possessing power to arrest without process any one known to be or suspected of being a member of the organization; and to feed, lodge or conceal a member was made a criminal offense punishable by fine and imprisonment, and informers were allowed one-half the fine. In spite of this drastic law, the Klan continued to actively operate in Tennessee for over six months.

Partly because of this law, and partly because of the fact that in many cases some of the "Dens" had gone beyond their instructions in coping with the situation, and were showing a tendency to get beyond the control of the men who were trying to conduct the movement honestly, but principally because the purpose of its regulation work had been accomplished and there remained no reason for its existence, General Forrest, in the latter part of February,

1869, issued a proclamation as Grand Wizard
declaring the Ku Klux Klan dissolved and disbanded.

The substance of his order is included in his
summary which reads:

"The Invisible Empire has accomplished the purpose
for which it was organized. Civil law now affords ample
protection to life, liberty and property; robbery and
lawlessness are no longer unrebuked; the better elements
of society are no longer in dread for the safety of their
property, their persons, and their families. The Grand
Wizard, being invested with power to determine questions
of paramount importance, in the exercise of the power so
conferred, now declares the Invisible Empire and all the
subdivisions thereof dissolved and disbanded forever."

Thus ended the second period of Ku Kluxism
in the South. A large number of "Dens," however, paid no attention to the order of General
Forrest, but continued to act independently, and
kept up their work until the late seventies.
The "Pale Faces," the "Constitutional Union
Guards," the "White Brotherhood," "White
League," and the "Knights of the White
Camelia" were also kept up for several years
after the organization of the Ku Klux Klan
was officially abandoned, it being very likely
that many of the Klan units joined in with
these movements. It is generally understood
that the work done by these organizations, and
by the irresponsible people who still used the name
of the old Klan, was more reckless and violent in
its character and was the cause of more bloodshed
than the original movement. At any rate there

was less justification for the movement after 1870
than in the first years of the reconstruction.

Ku Kluxism occupied a great deal of attention of Congress in 1870, 1871 and in 1872, the
President issued proclamations against it backed
by the army, committees were sent by Congress
to visit every section of the South, volumes of
testimony were taken, hundreds of speeches
were made, in some instances martial law was
declared, and a drastic act was passed by
Congress intended to check the movement.
It went on, however, until the Federal troops
were withdrawn, the carpetbaggers left the
country, and all of the State governments were
in the control of the white men of the South.

Mr. Gregory in summing up the whole Ku
Klux movement said:

"Did the end aimed at and accomplished by the Ku
Klux Klan justify the movement?   The opinion of the
writer is that the movement was fully justified, though
he of course does not approve of the crimes and excesses
incident to it.

"The abuses under which the American colonies of
England revolted in 1776 were mere child's play compared
to those borne by the South during the period of reconstruction, and the success of the later movement as a
justification of a last resort to revolutionary methods
was as pronounced as that of the former.

"The Ku Klux machine has been stored away in the
Battle Abbey of the nation as obsolete, we trust, as the
causes which produced it; it will stand there for all time
as a reminder of how useless is the prostitution of forms
of law in an effort to do that which is essentially unlawful, but it will also remain an eternal suggestion to the
vigilance committee and the regulator."

CHAPTER XI

THE PRESCRIPT OF THE OLD KLAN

IN the study of the original Ku Klux Klan, it is fortunate that there have been preserved documents which fully set forth its structure and composition, and these documents demonstrate conclusively that the modern organization has no claim whatever to recognition as the "genuine original Ku Klux." The most important of these documents is the "prescript" or constitution of the old Klan.

In its early stages, the old organization adopted a "Prescript," but this was in 1867 revised and amended, and the second document became the law of the organization, under which it functioned until it was disbanded. When General Forrest issued his order disbanding the Ku Klux Klan, all copies of the revised and amended prescript were ordered destroyed. One copy escaped destruction and is now in the library of Columbia University where it is carefully preserved as a valuable historic paper. As an exhibit in the case against the present organization, I give the "Prescript" in full. It is a booklet of twenty-four pages, and at the top of each page is a Latin quotation. Without attempting to follow the typography of the original text, I am reproducing it as a continuous document, placing the quotations where they appear in the booklet, as follows:

"PRESCRIPT"

Exact copy of the Revised and Amended
Prescript
of the
ORDER
of the
*

*   *

"Damnant   quod   intelligent"

"APPELLATION"

This organization shall by styled and denominated, The Order of * * *

"CREED"

"We, the Order of the * * * , reverentially acknowledge the majesty and supremacy of the Divine Being, and recognize the goodness and providence of the same. And we recognize our relation to the United States Government, the supremacy of the Constitution, the Constitutional Laws thereof, and the union of States thereunder.

"CHARACTER AND OBJECTS OF THE ORDER

"This is an institution of Chivalry, Humanity, Mercy, and Patriotism embodying in its genius and its principles all that is chivalric in conduct, noble in sentiment, generous in manhood, and patriotic in purpose; its object being,

"First: To protect the weak, the innocent, and the defenseless from the indignities, wrongs, and outrages of the lawless, the violent, and the brutal; to relieve the injured and oppressed; to succor the suffering and unfortunate, and especially the widows and orphans of Confederate Soldiers.

"Second: To protect and defend the Constitution of the United States and all laws passed in conformity thereto, and to protect the States and the people thereof from all invasion from any source whatever (*Nec scire fas est omnia*).

"Third: To aid and assist in the execution of all constitutional laws, and to protect the people from unlawful seizure, and from trial except by their peers in conformity to the laws of the land.

ARTICLE I

TITLES

"*Section 1*. The officers of the Order shall consist of a Grand Wizard of the Empire, and his ten Genii; a Grand Dragon of the realm, and his eight Hydras; a Grand Titan of the Dominion, and his six Furies; a Grand Giant of the Province, and his four Goblins; a Grand Cyclops of the Den, and his two Night Hawks; a Grand Magi, a Grand Monk, a Grand Scribe, a Grand Exchequer, a Grand Turk, and a Grand Sentinel.

"*Section 2*. The body politic of the Order shall be known and designated as 'Ghouls.'

ARTICLE II
Territory and Its Divisions

"*Section 1.* The territory embraced within the jurisdiction of this Order shall be coterminous with the States of Maryland, Virginia, North Carolina, South Carolina, Georgia, Florida, Alabama, Mississippi, Louisiana, Texas, Arkansas, Missouri, Kentucky and Tennessee; all combined constituting the Empire.

"*Section 2.* The Empire shall be divided into four departments, the first to be styled the Realm, and coterminous with the boundaries of the several States; the second to be styled the Dominion and (*Amici humani generis*) to be coterminous with such counties as the Grand Dragons of the several Realms may assign to the charge of the Grand Titan; the third to be styled the Province, and to be coterminous with the several counties; provided, the Grand Titan may, when he deems it necessary, assign two Grand Giants to one Province, prescribing at the same time the jurisdiction of each. The fourth department to be styled the Den, and shall embrace such part of a Province as the Grand Giant shall assign to the charge of a Grand Cyclops.

ARTICLE III
Powers and Duties of Officers
Grand Wizard

"*Section 1.* The Grand Wizard, who is the supreme officer of the Empire, shall have power,

and he shall be required to appoint Grand
Dragons for the different Realms of the Empire;
and he shall have power to appoint his Genii;
also a Grand Scribe and a Grand Exchequer
for his department, and he shall have the sole
power to issue copies of this "Prescript,"
through his Subalterns, for the organization
and dissemination of the Order; and when a
question of paramount importance to the interests or prosperity of the Order arises, not provided for in this "Prescript," he shall have the
power to determine the question, and his decision
shall be final until the same shall be provided
for by amendment as hereinafter provided.
It shall be his duty to communicate with, and
receive reports from the Grand Dragons of
Realms as to the condition, strength, and
progress of the Order within their respective
Realms, and (*Quemcunque miserum videris,
hominem scias*) it shall further be his duty to
keep, by his Grand Scribe, a list of the names
(without any caption or explanation whatever)
of the Grand Dragons of the different Realms
of the Empire, and shall number such Realms
with the Arabic numerals 1, 2, 3 etc. *ad finem;*
and he shall direct his Grand Exchequer as to
the appropriation and disbursement he shall
make of the revenue of the Order that comes
to his hands.

Grand Dragon

"*Section 2.* The Grand Dragon, who is the
chief officer of the Realm, shall have power,

and he shall be required to appoint and instruct a Grand Titan for each Dominion of his realm (such Dominion not to exceed three in number for any Congressional District), said appointments being subject to the approval of the Grand Wizard of the Empire. He shall have power to appoint his Hydras; also a Grand Scribe and a Grand Exchequer for his department.

It shall be his duty to report to the Grand Wizard, when required by that officer, the condition, strength, efficiency, and progress of the Order within his Realm, and to transmit, through the Grand Titan, or other authorized sources, to the Order, all information, intelligence, or instruction conveyed to him by the Grand Wizard for that purpose, and all such information or instructions as he may think will promote the interest and utility of the Order. He shall keep, by his Grand Scribe, a list of the names (without caption) of the Grand Titans of the different Dominions of his Realm, and shall report the same to the Grand Wizard when required, and (*Magna est veritas, et prevalebit*) shall number the Dominions of his Realm with the Arabic numerals 1, 2, 3, etc. *ad finem*. And he shall direct and instruct his Grand Exchequer as to the appropriation and disbursement he shall make of the revenue of the Order that comes to his hands.

Grand Titan

"*Section 3.* The Grand Titan, who is the chief officer of the Dominion, shall have power and he shall be required to appoint and instruct a Grand Giant for each Province of his Dominion such appointment, however, being subject to the approval of the Grand Dragon of the Realm. He shall have the power to appoint his Furies; also a Grand Scribe and a Grand Exchequer for his department. It shall be his duty to report to the Grand Dragon, when required by that officer, the condition, strength, efficiency, and progress of the order within his Dominion and to transmit through the Grand Giant, or other authorized channels, to the Order, all information, intelligence, instruction, or directions conveyed to him by the Grand Dragon for that purpose, and all such other information or instruction as he may think will enhance the interest or efficiency of the Order.

"He shall keep, by his Grand Scribe, a list of the names (without caption or explanation) of the Grand Giants of the different Provinces of his Dominion, and shall report the same to the Grand Dragon when required; and shall number the Provinces of his Dominion with the Arabic numerals 1, 2, 3, etc. *ad finem.* And he shall direct and instruct his Grand Exchequer as to the appropriation and disbursement he shall make of the revenue of the Order that comes to his hands. (*Ne tentes aut perfice.*)

Grand Giant

"*Section 4.* The Grand Giant, who is the chief officer of the Province, shall have power, and he is required, to appoint and instruct a Grand Cyclops for each Den of his Province, and such appointment, however, being subject to the approval of the Grand Titan of the Dominion. And he shall have the further power to appoint his Goblins; also a Grand Scribe and a Grand Exchequer for his department.

It shall be his duty to supervise and administer general and special instructions in the organization and establishment of the Order within his Province, and to report to the Grand Titan, when required by that officer, the condition, strength and progress of the Order within his Province, and to transmit through the Grand Cyclops, or other legitimate sources, to the Order, all information, intelligence, instruction, or directions conveyed to him by the Grand Titan or other higher authority for that purpose, and all such other information or instruction as he may think would advance the purposes or prosperity of the Order. He shall keep, by his Grand Scribe, a list of the names (without caption or explanation) of the Grand Cyclops of the various Dens of his Province, and shall report the same to the Grand Titan when required; and shall number the Dens of his Province with the Arabic numerals 1, 2, 3, etc. *ad finem.* He shall determine and limit the number of Dens to be organized and estab-

lished in his Province; and shall direct and
instruct his Grand Exchequer as to the appropriation and disbursement he shall make of the
revenue of the Order that comes to his hands.
(*Quid faciendum?*)

Grand Cyclops

"*Section 5.* The Grand Cyclops, who is the
chief officer of the Den, shall have power to
appoint his Night Hawks, his Grand Scribe, his
Grand Turk, his Grand Exchequer, and his
Grand Sentinel. And for small offenses he may
punish any member by fine, and may reprimand him for the same. And he is further
empowered to admonish and reprimand his
Den, or any of the members thereof, for any
imprudence, irregularity, or transgression whenever he may think that the interests, welfare,
reputation or safety of the Order demands it.
It shall be his duty to take charge of his Den
under the instruction and with the assistance
(when practicable) of the Grand Giant, and
in accordance with and in conformity to the
provisions of this Prescript, a copy of which
shall in all cases be obtained before the formation of a Den begins. It shall further be his
duty to appoint all regular meetings of his
Den, and to preside at the same; to appoint
irregular meetings when he deems it expedient;
to preserve order and enforce discipline in
his Den; to impose fines for irregularities or
disobedience of orders; and to receive and

initiate candidates for admission into the Order,
after the same shall have been pronounced
competent and worthy to become members,
by the Investigating Committee hereinafter
provided for. And it shall further be his duty
to make a quarterly report to the Grand Giant
of the condition, strength, efficiency and progress
of his Den, and shall communicate to the
Officers and Ghouls of his Den all information,
intelligence, instruction or direction conveyed
to him by the Grand Giant or other higher
authority for that (*Fiat justicia coelum*) purpose;
and shall from time to time administer all
other counsel, instruction, or direction, as in
his sound discretion, will conduce to the interests,
and more effectually accomplish, the real objects
and designs of the Order.

Grand Magi

"*Section 6*. It shall be the duty of the Grand
Magi, who is the second officer in authority of
the Den, to assist the Grand Cyclops, and to
obey all the orders of that officer; to preside
at all meetings in the Den, in the absence of the
Grand Cyclops; and to discharge during his
absence all the duties and exercise all the powers
and authority of that officer.

Grand Monk

Section 7. It shall be the duty of the Grand
Monk, who is the third officer of the Den, to
assist and obey all the orders of the Grand Magi;

and in the absence of both of these officers he
shall preside at and conduct the meetings in the
Den, and shall discharge all the duties, and
exercise all the powers and authority of the
Grand Cyclops.

Grand Exchequer

"*Section 8.* It shall be the duty of the Grand
Exchequers of all the different departments to
keep a correct account of all the revenue of
the Order that comes to their hands, and of all
paid out by them; and shall make no appropriation or disbursement of the same except under
the orders and direction of (*Dormitus aliquando
jus, moritus nunquam*) the chief officer of their
respective departments. And it shall further
be the duty of the Exchequers of Dens to collect
the initiation fees, and all fines imposed by the
Grand Cyclops, or the officer discharging his
functions.

Grand Turk

"*Section 9.* It shall be the duty of the Grand
Turk, who is the executive officer of the Grand
Cyclops, to notify the officers and Ghouls of the
Den of all informal or irregular meetings
appointed by the Grand Cyclops, and to obey
and execute all the orders of that officer in the
control and government of his Den. It shall
further be his duty to receive and question
at the outpost, all candidates for admission
into the order and shall there administer the
preliminary obligation required, and then con-

duct such candidate or candidates to the Grand
Cyclops, and to assist him in the initiation of
the same.

Grand Scribe

"*Section 10.* It shall be the duty of the
Grand Scribes of the different Departments to
conduct the correspondence and write the
orders of the Chiefs of their Departments when
required. And it shall further be the duty of the
Grand Scribes of Dens to keep a list of the names
(without any caption or explanation whatever)
of the officers and Ghouls of the Den, to call the
roll at all meetings, and to make the quarterly
reports under the direction and instruction of
the Grand Cyclops. (*Quieta non movere.*)

Grand Sentinel

"*Section 11.* It shall be the duty of the Grand
Sentinel to take charge of post and instruct the
Grand Guard, under the direction and orders
of the Grand Cyclops, and to relieve and dis-
miss the same when directed by that officer.

The Staff

"*Section 12.* The Genii shall constitute the
staff of the Grand Wizard; the Hydras, that of
the Grand Dragon; the Furies, that of the
Grand Titan; and the Night-Hawks that of the
Grand Cyclops.

Removal

"*Section 13.* For any just, reasonable, and
substantial cause, any appointee may be

removed by the authority that appointed him, and his place supplied by another appointment.

ARTICLE IV
ELECTION OF OFFICERS

"*Section 1.* The Grand Wizard shall be elected biennially by the Grand Dragons of Realms. The first election for this office to take place on the first Monday in May, 1870 (a Grand Wizard having been created by the original 'Prescript,' to serve three years from the first Monday in May, 1867); all subsequent elections to take place every two years thereafter. And the incumbent Grand Wizard shall notify the Grand Dragons of the different Realms, at least six months before said election at what time (*Quid verum atque decens*) and place the same shall be held; a majority vote of all the Grand Dragons *present* being necessary and sufficient to elect a Grand Wizard. Such election shall be by ballot and shall be held by three Commissioners appointed by the Grand Wizard for that purpose; and in the event of a tie, the Grand Wizard shall have the casting vote.

"*Section 2.* The Grand Magi and the Grand Monk of Dens shall be elected annually by the Ghouls of Dens; and the first election for these officers may take place as soon as ten Ghouls have been initiated for the formation of a Den. All subsequent elections to take place every year thereafter.

"*Section 3.* In the event of a vacancy in the

office of Grand Wizard, by death, resignation, removal, or otherwise, the senior Grand Dragon of the Empire shall immediately assume and enter upon the discharge of the duties of the Grand Wizard, and shall exercise the powers and perform the duties of said office until the same shall be filled by election; and the said Senior Grand Dragon, as soon as practicable after the happening of such vacancy, shall call a convention of the Grand Dragons of the Realms, to be held at such time and place as in his discretion he may deem most convenient and proper. *Provided,* however, that the time for assembling such convention for the election of a Grand Wizard shall in no case exceed six months from the time such vacancy occurred; and in the event of a vacancy in any other office the same shall immediately be filled in the manner hereinbefore mentioned.

"*Section 4.* The Officers heretofore elected or appointed may retain their offices during the time for (*Art est colare artem*) which they have been so elected or appointed, at the expiration of which time said offices shall be filled as hereinbefore provided.

ARTICLE V
JUDICIARY

"*Section 1.* The Tribunal of Justice of this Order shall consist of a court at the Headquarters of the Empire, the Realm, the Dominion, the Province, and the Den, to be appointed by the Chiefs of the several departments.

"*Section 2.* The Court at the Headquarters of the Empire shall consist of three Judges for the trial of Grand Dragons and the Officers and attaches belonging to the Headquarters of the Empire.

"*Section 3.* The Court at the Headquarters of the Realm shall consist of three Judges for trial of Grand Titans, and the Officers and attaches belonging to the Headquarters of the Realm.

"*Section 4.* The Court at the Headquarters of the Dominion shall consist of three Judges for the trial of Grand Giants, and the Officers and attaches belonging to the Headquarters of the Dominion.

"*Section 5.* The court at the Headquarters of the Province shall consist of five Judges for the trial of Grand Cyclops, the Grand Magis, the Grand Monks, and the Grand Exchequers of Dens, and the officers and attaches belonging to the Headquarters of the Province.

"*Section 6.* The Court at the Headquarters of the Den shall consist of seven Judges from (*Nusquam tuta fides*) the Den for the trial of Ghouls and the Officers belonging to the Headquarters of the Den.

"*Section 7.* The Tribunal for the trial of the Grand Wizard shall be composed of at least seven Grand Dragons, to be convened by the senior Grand Dragon upon charges being preferred against the Grand Wizard; which Tribunal shall be organized and presided over by the senior Grand Dragon *present;* and if they find the accused guilty they shall prescribe the penalty, and the senior Grand Dragon of the Empire shall cause the same to be executed.

"*Section 8.* The aforesaid Courts shall summon the accused and witnesses for and against him, and if found guilty, they shall prescribe the penalty, and the Officers convening the Court shall cause the same to be executed. *Provided,* the accused shall always have the right of appeal to the next court above, whose decision shall be final.

"*Section 9.* The Judges constituting the aforesaid Courts shall be selected with reference to their intelligence, integrity, and fair-mindedness and shall render their verdict without prejudice, favor, partiality, or affection, and shall be so sworn, upon the organization of the Court; and shall further be sworn to administer evenhanded justice.

"*Section 10.* The several courts herein provided for shall be governed in their deliberations, proceedings, and judgments by the rules and regulations governing the proceedings of regular courts-martial. (*Fide non armis.*)

ARTICLE VI

Revenue

"*Section 1.* The revenue of this order shall be derived as follows: For every copy of this

'Prescript' issued to Dens $10 will be required; $2.00 of which shall go into the hands of the Grand Exchequer of the Grand Giant; $2.00 into the hands of the Grand Exchequer of the Grand Titan; $2.00 into the hands of the Grand Exchequer of the Grand Dragon, and the remaining $4.00 into the hands of the Grand Exchequer of the Grand Wizard.

"*Section 2.* A further source of revenue to the Empire shall be ten per cent of all the revenue of the Realms, and a tax upon realms when the Grand Wizard shall deem it necessary and indispensable to levy same.

Section 3. "A further source of revenue to Realms shall be ten per cent of all the revenue of Dominions, and a tax upon Dominions when the Grand Dragon shall deem it necessary and indispensable to levy the same.

"*Section 4.* A further source of revenue to Dominions shall be ten per cent of all the revenue of Provinces, and a tax upon Provinces when the Grand Titan shall deem such tax necessary and indispensable.

"*Section 5.* A further source of revenue to Provinces shall be ten per cent of all the revenue of Dens, and a tax upon Dens when the Grand Giant shall deem such tax necessary and indispensable. (*Dat Deus hisquoque finem.*)

Section 6. The source of revenue to Dens shall be the initiation fees, fines, and a *per capita* tax, whenever the Grand Cyclops shall deem such tax necessary and indispensable to the interests and objects of the Order.

"*Section 7.* All the revenue obtained in the manner aforesaid shall be for the *exclusive* benefit of the Order, and shall be appropriated to the dissemination of the same and to the creation of a fund to meet any disbursement that it may become necessary to make to accomplish the objects of the Order and to secure the protection of the same.

ARTICLE VII
ELIGIBILITY FOR MEMBERSHIP

"*Section 1.* No one shall be presented for admission into the Order until he shall have first been recommended by some friend or intimate who *is* a member, to the Investigation Committee (which shall be composed of the Grand Cyclops, the Grand Magi, and the Grand Monk), and who shall have investigated his antecedents and his past and present standing and connections, and after such investigation, shall have pronounced him competent and worthy to become a member. *Provided,* no one shall be presented for admission into, or become a member of this Order, who shall not have attained the age of eighteen years.

"*Section 2.* No one shall become a member of this Order unless he shall *voluntarily* take the following oaths or obligations, and shall *satisfactorily* answer the following interrogatories, with (*Cessante causa, cessat effectus*) his right hand raised to heaven, and his left hand resting on the Bible.

Preliminary Obligation

"I ————— solemnly swear or affirm that I will never reveal anything that I may this day (or night) learn concerning the Order of the * * * and that I will true answer make to such interrogatories as may be put to me touching my competency for admission into the same. So help me God."

Interrogatories To Be Asked

"*First*. Have you ever been rejected, upon application for membership in the * * * or have you ever been expelled from the same?

"*Second*. Are you now, or have you ever been, a member of the Radical Republican party, or either of the organizations known as the 'Loyal League' and the 'Grand Army of the Republic'?

"*Third*. Are you opposed to the principles and policy of the Radical Party, and to the Loyal League, and the Grand Army of the Republic, so far as you are informed of the character and purposes of these organizations?

"*Fourth*. Did you belong to the Federal Army during the late war, and fight against the South during the existence of the same?

"*Fifth*. Are you opposed to negro equality, both social and political?

"*Sixth.* Are you in favor of a white man's government in this country?

"*Seventh.* Are you in favor of Constitutional liberty and a Government of equitable laws instead of a Government of violence and oppression? (*Cave quid, dicis, quando, et cui*).

"*Eighth.* Are you in favor of maintaining the constitutional rights of the South?

"*Ninth.* Are you in favor of the re-enfranchisement and emancipation of the white men of the South, and the restitution of the Southern people to all their rights, alike proprietary, civil and political?

"*Tenth.* Do you believe in the inalienable right of self-preservation of the people against the exercise of arbitrary and unlicensed power?

"If the foregoing interrogatories are satisfactorily answered, and the candidate desires to go further (after something of the character and nature of the Order has thus been indicated to him) and to be admitted to the benefits, mysteries, secrets, and purposes of the Order, he shall then be required to take the following final oath or obligation. But if said interrogatories are not satisfactorily answered, or the candidate declines to proceed further, he shall be discharged, after being solemnly admonished by the initiatory officer of the deep secrecy to which the oath already taken has bound him, and that the extreme penalty of the law will follow a violation of the same.

Final Obligation

"I ——————— of my own free will and accord,
and in the presence of Almighty God, do
solemnly swear or affirm, that I will never reveal
to any one, not even a member of the Order of
the * * * by any intimation, sign, symbol, word
or act, or in any (*Nemo tenetur seipsum accura*)
other manner whatever, any of the secrets, signs,
grip, pass words, or mysteries of the Order of
the * * *, or that I am a member of the same,
or that I know any one who *is* a member; and
that I will abide by the Prescript and Edicts
of the Order of the * * * So help me God.

"The initiating officer will then proceed to
explain to the new member the character and
objects of the Order, and introduce him to the
mysteries and secrets of the same and shall read
to him this Prescript and the Edicts thereof,
or present the same to him for personal perusal.

ARTICLE VIII

Amendments

"This Prescript or any part of the Edicts
thereof shall never be changed, except by a
two-thirds vote of the Grand Dragons of the
Realms, in convention assembled, and at which
convention the Grand Wizard shall preside
and be entitled to a vote. And upon the application of a majority of the Grand Dragons for
that purpose, the Grand Wizard shall call and
appoint the time and place for said convention,

which, when assembled, shall proceed to make such modifications and amendments as it may think will promote the interest, enlarge the utility, and more thoroughly effectuate the purposes of the Order.

ARTICLE IX

INTERDICTION

"The origin, mysteries and Ritual of this Order shall never be written, but the same shall be communicated orally."

(Deo adjuvante, non timendum)

ARTICLE X

"EDICTS"

"1. No one shall become a member of a distant Den where there is a Den established and in operation in his own immediate vicinity; nor shall any one become a member of any Den, or of this Order in any way, after he shall have been once rejected upon application.

"2. No Den, or officer, or member, or members thereof, shall operate beyond their prescribed limits, unless invited or ordered by the proper authority to do so.

"3. No member shall be allowed to take any intoxicating spirits to any meeting of the Den; nor shall any member be allowed to attend a meeting while intoxicated; and for every appearance at a meeting in such condition he shall be fined the sum of not less than one nor more than five dollars to go into the revenue of the Order.

"4. Any member may be expelled from the Order by a majority vote of the officers and Ghouls of the Den to which he belongs; and if after such expulsion, such member shall assume any of the duties, regalia, or insignia of the Order, or in any way claim to be a member of the same, he shall be punished. His obligation of secrecy shall be as binding upon him after his expulsion as before, and for any revelation made by him thereafter he shall be held account-able in the same manner as if he were a member.

"5. Upon the expulsion of any member from the Order, the Grand Cyclops, or any officer acting in (*Spectemus agendo*) his stead, shall immediately report the same to the Grand Giant of the Province, who shall cause the fact to be made known and read in each Den of his Province, and shall transmit the same, through the proper channels, to the Grand Dragon of the Realm who shall cause it to be published to every Den in the Realm, and shall notify the Grand Dragons of contiguous Realms of the same.

"6. Every Grand Cyclops shall read, or cause to be read, this Prescript and these Edicts to his Den, at least once in every month; and shall read them to each new member when he is initiated, or present the same to him for his personal perusal.

"7. The initiation fee of this Order shall be one dollar, to be paid when the candidate is initiated and received into the Order.

"8. Dens may make such additional Edicts for their control and government as they may deem requisite and necessary, *Provided*, no Edict shall be made to conflict with any of the provisions or Edicts of this Prescript.

"9. The most profound and rigid secrecy concerning any and everything that relates to the Order shall at all times be maintained.

"10. Any member who shall reveal or betray the secrets of this Order shall suffer the supreme penalty.

ADMONITION

"Hush! thou art not to utter what I am; bethink thee, it was our covenant!

(*Nemo nos impune lacessit*)

REGISTER
I

1. Dismal	7. Painful
2. Mystic	8. Portentious
3. Stormy	9. Fading
4. Peculiar	10. Melancholy
5. Blooming	11. Glorious
6. Brilliant	12. Gloomy

II

I White, II Green, III Yellow, IV Amber, V Purple, VI Crimson, VII Emerald.

III

1. Fearful	7. Hideous
2. Startling	8. Frightful
3. Wonderful	9. Awful
4. Alarming	10. Horrible
5. Mournful	11. Dreadful
6. Appalling	12. Last

IV

CUMBERLAND
Ad unum omnes

L'ENVOI

"To the lovers of law and order, peace and justice, we send greeting; and to the shades of the venerated dead we affectionately dedicate the Order of the * * *

RESURGAMUS

(Author's note: The "register" above given, was used by the original Ku Klux Klan as a code to indicate the day and hour for meeting. The first section indicated half of the hours in the day, the second section the days of the week, and the third section the remaining twelve hours. The word "Cumberland" seems to have been a general code expression.)

CHAPTER XII

COMPARISON OF OLD AND NEW KLANS

HAVING briefly sketched the causes which led up to the organization of the original Ku Klux Klan, and to some extent the actual work accomplished by that Order, and having shown in detail the rules and regulations governing it in the form of its "Revised and Amended Prescript," we can easily see by a comparison of the old and new organizations that the claim of the latter that it is "the genuine and original Klan" is a historical fraud. The modern system, while appropriating to itself the name, regalia, and some of the nomenclature of the original Klan, is different in conception, organization and purpose.

In certain respects the character of the two organizations is about the same. General Forrest when called before a Congressional investigating committee in 1872, stated that the Ku Klux Klan was a political-military organization with branches in every voting place in the South, and that, in addition to its work as a regulator of the peace, it was also engaged in the task of fighting the Republican Party at the polls. The modern organization states in its secret constitution that it is a military organization, and a

study of its oath and its literature as herein
presented proves conclusively that it is also a
political organization, which intends, when it
develops the necessary strength, to drive from
public office in the United States every Jew,
Catholic, and foreign-born citizen.

The original Klan presents in its defense that
it policed and enforced law in a badly demoralized country, brought order out of chaos, and
protected the widow and the orphan. The new
Klan has at times given out a few charities,
largely for advertising purposes, and whenever
this has been done has sought as much publicity
as possible from its work. It has announced
that it intends to protect the womanhood of
the country, and one Klan in Texas has issued
a warning that "husbands must spend more
time with their own wives," without, however,
consulting the wishes of either of the parties to
ascertain if the same was agreeable. As far
as has been printed in the newspapers, however,
the Klan in its eagerness to protect womanhood
has not discovered and punished the masked and
white-robed people who stripped Mrs. Beulah
Brown of her clothing at Tenasha, Tex.,
whipped her and covered her body with tar
and feathers.

The two organizations have something in
common in the proven cases of violence that
have been reported in the public prints. According to the statements of writers, who were members of the old Klan, there were men in the

organization who acted unwisely and selfishly, and who committed acts of violence that were impossible to control. Precisely the same situation has already developed in the United States today and the "Emperor" of the "Invisible Empire" has had to discipline three of his chartered Klans for proven acts of lawlessness. There is another point of similarity in the two systems. The old Klan had hardly started its work of wearing disguises to regulate public affairs when there sprang up imitators who used similar disguises to aid them in performing acts of viciousness and crime. These men were not members of the Klan and did things that had neither the sanction nor approval of the Klan, yet their acts showed that the wearing of disguises by the old Klan tended to promote lawlessness and crime in others. As will be shown later there has been, since the modern Klan was organized, an epidemic of crime in the South, usually committed by men wearing disguises. Whether these acts have actually been done by Klansmen or by imitators, it shows nevertheless that the admitted right of one class to go about disguised puts the community at the mercy of any class that chooses to employ similar tactics.

In spite of these resemblances, however, the difference between the old Ku Klux Klan and the new is appalling. One of the first questions that presents itself is, "What is the necessity at the present time for such an organization?"

The student of American history — in view of
the abnormal political situation in the Southern
States during the Reconstruction Period —
can readily understand how and why such an
organization should have come into existence,
and its justification lies solely in the necessity
of some agency to cope with the social upheaval
of that time. Public opinion in America today,
as reflected by the editorial comments of a
vast majority of the leading newspapers, is
practically unanimous in the view that there is
absolutely nothing in our present system of
government that would justify the existence of
any kind of extra-legal Ku Klux organization.
Every state in the Union has a constitution
which provides for the creation and maintenance
of legislative, judicial, and executive branches,
and in every State these branches are performing
their regularly constituted functions. None of
them is perfect; none of them ever will be.
At the same time, the machinery is there, is
being handled well, and there are but few
complaints against non-enforcement of the law,
except in some Southern States where men are
going about in disguise terrorizing the community. The Southern States are every one
governed by white men. White men make their
laws; white men enforce their laws; and white
men sit upon the bench and interpret their
laws. There is no danger in the South of a repetition of the scenes of the Reconstruction, and
no danger whatever of the "White Supremacy"

of the South being destroyed or set aside unless
the same is done by white men, who, under the
false pretense of "pure Americanism," seek to
array white men against white men by the
stirring up of religious and racial hatred and
prejudice. Where then, is the necessity either
in the South or anywhere else in America for
this modern Ku Klux monstrosity? From a
standpoint of necessity, neither the facts of
history nor modern conditions offer the remotest
excuse for its existence.

It is, however, the comparison of the *organization* of the old Klan and the new which refutes
absolutely the claim of the latter to any "genuineness" whatever. The "Prescript" of the
old Klan reads: "The Grand Wizard shall be
elected biennially by the Grand Dragons of
Realms." In the secret constitution of the new
Klan it is provided that the Imperial Wizard
shall hold his office for life, and can only be
removed by the *unanimous* vote of his hand-
picked Imperial Kloncilium.

Another important and interesting comparison
is that of the personalities of the two heads of
the organizations. When the convention was
held at Nashville, Tenn., in 1867, for the
purpose of choosing a Grand Wizard, it selected
Gen. Nathan Bedford Forrest, one of the
most distinguished and capable officers in the
late Confederate army, and recognized today
among military students as one of the foremost
cavalry leaders of all times. General Forrest

was selected for his ability, his integrity, his
unselfish devotion to the Southern people, and
his desire to aid them in a great crisis. A careful
search of every available record fails to reveal
that he ever received one penny as compensation for his labors, or that his office as Grand
Wizard ever brought him any gifts, perquisites,
or emoluments. His military title was unim-
peached, his last commission being that of
lieutenant-general. He never called himself
"Emperor," never signed any of his official
orders as "His Majesty," and never assumed
any of the titles or styles of royalty. He was a
plain, unassuming soldier and gentleman, who,
having a great task to perform, did his work
gratuitiously and from motives of patriotism
only, and then, the work having been completed,
disbanded his organization and retired.

What a marked contrast to the gallant Forrest
is "Colonel" (?) William Joseph Simmons,
Imperial Wizard, "Emperor" of the "Invisible
Empire," Knights of the Ku Klux Klan, Inc.
I can find no record of any military service that
gives him privilege to use the honorable title of
"Colonel," a title that has been won by American soldiers by virtue of hard service in the
army and by desperate deeds of valor on the
field of battle. Where then did "His Majesty"
get the right to use this military title? According to the *Literary Digest*, "his friends bestowed
it upon him."

Forrest, as far as can be ascertained, served his

country for patriotism; "Emperor" Simmons, on the other hand, is promoting the cause of "pure Americanism" for cash. Prior to his elevation to the responsible position of "Emperor" of the whole United States he was, among other activities, a professor of history at Lanier College in the good state of Georgia. He is also said to have been a Methodist exhorter earlier in his career. So far as the general public is informed, the remuneration of professors in our colleges and universities, even the greatest, is not particularly high. As Lanier College is a small institution that has had to struggle along in the face of more or less poor circumstances, it is not unreasonable to suppose that it is no exception to the general rule. In August, 1921, the newspapers reported that it had been taken over by the Ku Klux Klan, and that "Emperor" Simmons, "in addition to his other duties" would be its President. It is reasonably safe to say that the average income of "His Majesty" during his career as an educator could not have exceeded $2500 a year. Behold, however, the great change that comes with elevation to the Imperial Throne: "Friends of 'Colonel(?)' Simmons," at the Klonklave of the Klan which was held in Atlanta, in May, 1921, presented him with a $25,000 home on Peachtree Street — Atlanta's fashionable thoroughfare — together with handsome furniture.

In addition to this wonderful munificence of his "friends"— whoever they were — he is also paid a salary, which according to the "Emperor" himself is $1000 a month, and recently his hand-picked Kloncilium voted him $25,000 back pay. This stipend is augmented by the fact that the secret constitution provides that the "Imperial Wizard" shall also be the "Supreme Kleagle," and that he shall be entitled to "appropriate to himself" the entire ten-dollar "donations" paid by any members he may choose to solicit. Since the ordinary garden variety of Kleagle, with only four dollars "rake-off," can make a very tidy sum by selling memberships, the reader can draw his own conclusions as to the possible selling ability of the chief monarch. There is also the Gate City Manufacturing Company with its enormous revenue from the sale of robes, the Searchlight Publishing Company, the Clarke Realty Company, and Lanier College, which are interlocking corporations or business concerns conducted by persons connected with the Ku Klux Klan. Where the revenue derived from these enterprises goes has not been reported in the newspapers. The only thing made public in connection with them was the statement that the "Emperor" had been elected President of Lanier College. College presidents are usually paid salaries. When one thinks of the unpaid Forrest and the trying problems he solved, one can scarcely suppress a feeling of disgust in the effrontery of this man of modern times, who declares that this "is the genuine original Klan," and that he is engaged

in the work of "pure Americanism." Why,
the man doesn't know what pure Americanism
is!

The most important differentiation, however,
between the old Ku Klux Klan and its spurious
successor is the character of their membership.
It will be recalled upon a study of both systems
that in each candidates were required to answer
satisfactorily ten qualifying interrogatories before
being finally accepted for membership. Let us
compare these together.

ORIGINAL KLAN

"1. Have you ever been
rejected, upon application
for membership in * * *
or have you ever been
expelled from the same?

"2. Are you now, or
have you ever been, a
member of the Radical
Republican Party, or either
of the organizations known
as the Loyal League and
the Grand Army of the
Republic?

"3. Are you opposed to
the principles of the Radical
Party, and to the Loyal
League, and the Grand
Army of the Republic, so
far as you are informed of
the character and purposes
of these organizations?

MODERN KLAN

"1. Is the motive prompt-
ing your ambition to be a
Klansman serious and un-
selfish?

"2. Are you a native
born, white, Gentile American citizen?

"3. Are you absolutely
opposed to and free of any
allegiance of any nature to
any cause, government,
people, sect or ruler that
is foreign to the United
States of America?

"4. Did you belong to the Federal Army during the late war, and fight against the South during the existence of the same?

"5. Are you opposed to negro equality, both social and political?

"6. Are you in favor of a white man's government in this country?

"7. Are you in favor of constitutional liberty and a Government of equitable laws instead of a Government of violence and oppression?

"8. Are you in favor of maintaining the constitutional rights of the South?

"9. Are you in favor of the re-enfranchisement of the white men of the South and the restitution of the Southern people to all their rights, alike proprietary, civil and political?

"4. Do you believe in the tenets of the Christian religion?

"5. Do you esteem the United States of America and its institutions above any other government, civil, political or ecclesiastical in the whole world?

"6. Will you, without mental reservation, take a solemn oath to defend, preserve and enforce same?

"7. Do you believe in clannishness, and will you faithfully practice same towards Klansmen?

"8. Do you believe in and will you faithfully strive for the eternal maintenance of white supremacy?

"9. Will you faithfully obey our constitution and laws, and conform willingly to all our usages, requirements and regulations?

"10. Do you believe in the inalienable right of self-preservation of the people against the exercise of arbitrary and unlicensed power?"

From the Prescript of the Original Klan.

"10. Can you be always depended on?"

From the "Kloran."

A careful reading of these requisites for membership in the two organizations fails to show, except as to the matter of "white supremacy," that there is the remotest resemblance between them. Nowhere in the "Prescript" of the original Klan, or in any printed publication relating to it, can there be discovered any restriction whatever against the Jew, the Catholic, or the foreign-born American citizen. On the contrary, old men, who claim to have been members of the original movement, state that Jews, Catholics and foreigners were members. The fact that the modern movement is anti-Catholic and anti-Semitic and is opposed to the admission of foreign-born citizens of the country brands it *ipso facto* as a historical fraud.

Another link in the chain of evidence against the modern organization lies in the provisions governing eligibility for membership. Article VII of the old "Prescript" reads:

"No one shall be presented for membership into the Order until he shall have first been recommended by some friend or intimate who *is* a member, to the Investigating Committee (which shall be composed of the Grand Cyclops, the Grand Magi, and the Grand Monk), and who shall have investigated his antecedents and his past and present standing and connections, and after such investigation, shall have pronounced him competent and worthy to become a member."

It is here observed that in the selection of members the old Klan exercised the utmost care and scrutiny, and endeavored to throw around the organization every possible safe-guard against the admission of undesirable characters. Even with precautions like those, men who were members of the Klan and left behind them written testimony declare that many men of bad character became connected with the order. How utterly different is the modern system with its indiscriminate solicita-tion of membership, with its advertising methods, its open and notorious canvassing, and its selling campaigns by means of literature, letters, motion pictures, agents and speakers.

Also, as far as the records show, there was no propagation department in the old Klan, no system of Kleagles, King Kleagles, Goblins, or Imperial Kleagle. All that is a Simmons innovation, designed to gather in large sums of money from a large number of people, money that goes mostly into the pockets of paid workers whose chief interest in the "noble cause" is that of plunder and not of patriotism. The initiation fee of the old Klan was the paltry sum of one dollar. The new Klan, in its great piety and altruism denies that it has an initia-tion fee at all. It claims that "citizenship" in

the "Invisible Empire" cannot be bought.
Accordingly it requires that before attaining
this delectable privilege, the "alien" must
make a "donation" of ten dollars. A "donation" covers a multitude of sins. Where a
victim makes a free-will offering to a "noble
cause" he can hardly claim afterwards that
his money has been taken from him under false
pretenses.

In August, 1921, it was announced that "the
Invisible Empire" had amended its constitution so that women would be eligible for membership. This is a further point of dissimilarity
between the two organizations, for while women
were of great assistance to the original Klansmen
in making robes and in giving information, the
more serious work was done by the actual
members who were men. In announcing that
women were to be admitted to membership the
"Emperor" said:

"*First.* The influence of women over the youth of the
land shapes the destiny of the nation, and it is in the
cradles of the American homes where the principles and
ideals of Americanism should first be instilled into the
minds and hearts of the young. To the preservation of
these principles the Knights of the Ku Klux Klan is
dedicated.

"*Second.* The loyalty of the women to the original
Klan of the Reconstruction period convinces us that as
members of the Klan today there will be equal loyalty
and devotion to the fundamental principles underlying
the Order.

"*Third.* We know women can keep a secret, because
they made with their fingers 160,000 robes for members

of the old Klan and not one of them ever disclosed the
identity of any man who wore one of those robes.

"It is through the influence of women today that we
have some of the strongest men in the Order. And the
time has come to give the women recognition and to
allow them to partake of the honor and glory of membership in the organization."

In his statement, however, the "Emperor"
failed to elucidate point Number Four, which
was no doubt the principal incentive that caused
the admission of women. Each lady Ku Klux
will be required to donate ten dollars to the
"noble cause," and the admission of women
doubles the number of "prospects" to whom
the Ku Klux "gold brick" can be peddled. It
is doubtful if the effort to "work" this new field
will prove successful, as the women of the
South are more or less antagonistic to the movement. The Daughters of the Confederacy of
Virginia, at a convention held in the spring of
1921, passed a resolution condemning the organization, and asking the Virginia authorities to
suppress it. It is hardly likely that the daughters
of the women who "made with their fingers
160,000 robes for the old Klan" would care to
become associated with the Gate City Manufacturing Company, which is selling robes to all
members at $6.50 a robe, with a handsome
profit on the side. Women, as a rule, are good
buyers, and it is hardly probable that they
will look upon membership in the "Invisible
Empire" as a bargain even at ten dollars.
Women are also the chief supporters of the

churches of the country, and it is doubtful
if they would care to go through a "Naturalization" ceremony that is a blasphemous and
sacriligious parody on the sacred and Holy rite
of baptism.

Another point of comparison between the
two organizations lies in the attitude of the old
Klan and the new in reference to allowing
members to study their constitutions. We
find, in the case of the original Klan, the following edict:

"Every Grand Cyclops shall read, or cause to be read,
this Prescript and these Edicts to his Den, at least once
in every month; and shall read them to each new member
when he is initiated, or present the same to him for his
personal perusal."

Here we have openness, frankness, and a
disposition to take every member into the con-
fidence of the Order, so that each Klansman,
at all times, would have an opportunity to study
and to understand the laws of the organization
under which he was working. During the time
I was an active member and worker in the
modern Ku Klux Klan, the constitution was a
secret document. Members under me repeatedly
asked for a copy of it, and I transmitted their
requests to my immediate superior who could
not comply with it for the reason that he had
never seen a copy of it himself. It was only
after he had served as King Kleagle of Tennessee
for six months that he was permitted to have
one copy for which he had to give an iron-clad

receipt. I was allowed to glance through the
booklet comprising the document, which afforded
me the opportunity of noting a few salient
points, but this happened just as I was leaving
the work. The officials of the organization
dare not permit the booklet I saw to be generally
circulated among their members.

As a final comparison of the two organizations it is interesting to note that the leader of
the old Klan recognized that it was brought
into being for the accomplishment of a specific,
a definite and a concrete purpose. It fulfilled
its mission, and as soon as it became evident
that this was the case General Forrest ordered
its disbandment. He stated that with the
courts properly functioning and the government
properly established, there was no longer any
need for the Klan's existence. The new Klan,
on the other hand, aside from taking money
away from the public, has not made any public
statement as to its real intentions. In some of
the pronouncements printed in the official
organ, there is an indication that the "citizens"
of the "Invisible Empire" generally understand
that the movement has a definite national
mission. It is a matter of serious conjecture
as to what kind of mission a secret, military,
"Invisible Empire" can have in the United
States. That there is no intention of disbanding
the organization is evident by the fact that
every attack made upon the system has so far
resulted in a redoubling of efforts by the propaga-

tion agents. Statements reiterating the idea of "pure Americanism" and giving expression to high-sounding and sanctimonious platitudes come in unending streams from the pen of the "Emperor," who brazenly insists that his organization intends to enforce law and order.

The old Ku Klux Klan has a very deep place in the hearts of the Southern people, and it holds the added glamour of being an organization about which little was known by the public up to a few years ago. Knowing this feeling, the promoters of the modern organization have worked overtime upon the sympathies of the South in fostering an entirely different proposition. No matter what may be the ultimate objects of this organization, its claims to "genuineness" are fraudulent. Some of the leading men of the South and most of the newspapers have detected the fraud, but a great many unthinking men have joined the new movement under the impression that they were becoming members of the old organization. These men, when they have learned the truth, and have taken the trouble to study for themselves what I have discovered, will, I believe, withdraw from the organization and denounce it for what it is — an historical fraud.

CHAPTER XIII

LAWLESSNESS AND CRIME

BEFORE presenting, for the thoughtful consideration of the reader, the facts to be set forth in this chapter, I submit for comparison certain portions of the Constitution of the United States, and the concluding portion of the "oath of allegiance" of the "Invisible Empire," Knights of the Ku Klux Klan.

The former consists of what is known as the "Bill of Rights," and read:

"The right of the people to be secure in their persons, houses, papers, and effects, *against unreasonable searches and seizures, shall not be violated,* and no warrants shall issue but upon probable cause, supported by oath or affirmation, and particularly describing the place to be searched, and the persons or things to be seized."

4th Amendment.

"No person shall be held to answer for a capital or other infamous crime unless on a presentment or indictment of a grand jury, except in cases arising in the land or naval forces, or in the militia, when in actual service, in time of war or public danger; nor shall any person be subject for the same offence to be twice put in jeopardy of life or limb; nor shall be compelled in any criminal case to be a witness against himself, *nor be deprived of life, liberty, or property, without due process of law;* nor shall prva te property be taken for public use without just compensation."

5th Amendment.

180

"*In all criminal prosecutions, the accused shall enjoy the right to speedy and public trial, by an impartial jury of the State and district wherein the crime shall have been committed, which districts shall have been previously ascertained by law, and to be informed of the nature and cause of the accusation; to be confronted with the witnesses against him: to have compulsory process for obtaining witnesses in his favor and to have the assistance of counsel in his defence.*"

6th Amendment.

"Excessive bail shall not be required, nor excessive fines imposed, *nor cruel and unusual punishments inflicted.*"

8th Amendment.

Having thoroughly studied the above portions of the Constitution of the United States, I now ask the reader to again study the concluding section of the Ku Klux oath:

"I swear that I will *most zealously and valiantly* shield and preserve, *by any and all justifiable means and methods,* the sacred constitutional rights and privileges of free public schools, free speech, free press, separation of church and state, *liberty, white supremacy,* just laws, and the *pursuit of happiness, against any encroachment, of any nature, by any person or persons,* political party or parties, *religious sect or people, native,* naturalized or foreign, *of any race, color,* creed, lineage, or tongue whatsoever."

Without comment, I merely offer the above extracts for study and comparison, and let the reader draw his own conclusions at the end of the chapter.

A large number of outrages, consisting of lawless acts of various kinds, have been reported in the newspapers as having been committed in the Southern States since early in 1921. Men have been taken from their homes and conveyed to lonely spots where they have been beaten, tarred, and feathered; women have been stripped of their clothing and covered with tar and feathers; some men have been boldly kidnapped in broad daylight and driven in automobiles to obscure places and there flogged; others have been whipped and mutilated for alleged immorality; a sixty-eight year old farmer was taken from his bed at night and beaten; an Episcopal clergyman was given a coat of tar and feathers; a New Yorker was shot and beaten; and, numerous "warnings" have been given both publicly and privately of "secret law enforcement" and of dire threats to "lay off" investigating the perpetrators.

In practically every instance of physical violence the criminal acts — committed in the name of "law and order"— have been perpetrated by men wearing disguises, described as white robes and masks.

In several cases of violence the white caps, after finishing their work, have left on the bodies of their victims the letters, "K. K. K." either burned on the body with acid, or printed on placards tied to the person maltreated. In cases where private warnings have been sent through the mails the same letters have been used, and in public warnings placards have been posted conspicuously bearing the actual name of the "Ku Klux Klan." Taking these facts into consideration, the evidence shows that the outrages were committed by men actuated with the spirit of Ku Kluxism, whether they were all committed officially by Klans in Simmons' organization or not. That remains to be determined, but one salient fact stands out very suspiciously and it is this: outrages committed in this fashion have only been epidemic since the "Invisible Empire" began its propagation in the States affected. In this connection, it might be well to recall the conversation I had with the King Kleagle of Tennessee in May, 1921.

Charters were about to be granted to three Klans in upper East Tennessee. I asked the King Kleagle this question:

"My people want to know what to do when they get their charters. What shall I tell them?"

"*Tell them to clean up their towns,*" *he replied.*

Among the first reported cases of violence on the part of masked men occurred in Atlanta, Ga., the headquarters of Ku Kluxism, the home of the "Invisible Empire." J. C. Thomas, a white man, received an anonymous letter advising him to "leave alone" a certain woman named Myers, upon penalty of action, but paid no attention to the warning. One night Thomas was enticed into entering a motor car in which were several strangers, the false representation being made that the "Chief of Police wanted to see him about some bad checks." The car was driven to Lakewood, an amusement park, and Thomas was ordered to get out. He refused to obey the order, drew his knife, and put up a fight, killing Fred Thompson, one of his abductors and wounding another. The Grand Jury of Fulton County failed to indict Thomas, but did indict two of his captors.

Simmons admitted that Thompson was a member of the Ku Klux Klan.

Numerous cases have been reported in Atlanta where threatening letters have been sent and received. A young Scotchman was threatened for making improper remarks about social equality, while a physician was warned on account of alleged neglect of his family. According to J. H. Leavitt, an Atlanta lawyer, who was himself threatened, not only was he himself marked for violence but included in the same category were Dr. C. B. Wilmer, the Episcopal clergyman and Ex-Senator Hoke Smith.

In Durham, North Carolina, a Greek restaurant proprietor received an anonymous warning signed "K. K. K." ordering him to leave town. It appeared that he had permitted the intermingling of the races in his place of business. The Greek refused to take the matter seriously, employed a lawyer and laughed the incident out of town. Nothing came of it.

After a careful and searching investigation made by the *New York World*, there have been disclosed a large number of cases of violence and lawlessness in the South, and a study of the synopsis of these cases is interesting. It will be noted that the majority of outrages have occurred in the State of Texas, where the masked regulators have been extremely active, and where the Ku Klux Klan is strongly organized. These outrages have been so numerous in Texas as to attract the attention of the entire country, and have caused an upheaval in the Lone Star State. Some of the really law-abiding Texas people, who do not believe in "invisible government" and irresponsible censorship of morals, have attempted to secure some sort of action at the hands of the Texas legislature. Their efforts in the summer of 1921 were not successful, one legislator even going so far as publicly to defend the Ku Klux Klan. Other indignant citizens announced that they would band themselves secretly together and wage war on Ku Kluxism.

A chronological summary of the published cases of lawlessness in the South, indicating the methods of Ku Kluxism, is as follows:

February 5, 1921.— In Houston, Texas, B. I. Hobbs, a lawyer, was seized, had his hair clipped and was ordered to leave town, the charge against him being "too close fraternization" with negroes. Hobbs then went to Alvin, Texas, a short distance away, and on February 8, 1921, was run out of that town by eight masked men.

March 3, 1921.— At Houston, Texas, J. La Fayette Cockrell, a negro dentist, was mutilated by masked men for alleged association with white women. A race riot nearly resulted from this attack.

March 7, 1921.— A. V. Hopkins, a merchant of Houston, Texas, was mutilated, tarred, and feathered for annoying high school girls.

April 1, 1921.— Alexander Johnson, a negro bell boy, of Dallas, Texas, was taken out by masked men, whipped, and the letters "K. K. K." burned on his forehead with acid. He was said to have associated with white women.

April 10, 1921.— Gus Beck, stock man, of Webster, Texas, was tied to a telegraph pole by masked men, beaten and left there all night.

April 10, 1921.— At Houston, Texas, J. S. Allen, prominent attorney, was seized in a crowded downtown street by masked men, and conveyed to the country in an automobile, He was there tarred and feathered. He was then returned to the city, and was dumped from a car into the middle of a street in the most prominent business section, in a nude condition except for the coating of tar and feathers. In the reports of the case there is no record of police interference.

April 15, 1921.— Bill Harris, negro bell boy, at Dallas, Texas, was beaten by masked men for alleged insult of white women.

April 26, 1921.— At Houston, Texas, J. W. McGee, an automobile salesman, was whipped by masked men for annoying high school girls.

May 1, 1921.— "Red" Kemp, a jitney driver, was whipped, tarred and feathered by twelve masked men at Goose Creek, Texas.

May 4, 1921.— Sam King, Marshal at Brenham, Texas, was tarred and feathered. He then resigned his office.

May 7, 1921.— At Beaumont, Texas, Dr. J. S. Paul was seized by fifteen masked men, whipped, tarred, and feathered and given forty-eight hours in which to leave the city. At the same time R. F. Scott, a Marine Corps veteran of Deweyville was given the same treatment. These two acts were publicly admitted by the Beaumont Klan, and their charter was revoked by "Emperor" Simmons.

May 20, 1921.— One thousand men marched through the streets of Dallas, Texas, at night, mounted and unmounted, all of them attired in the Ku Klux regalia. They carried a fiery cross, and several banners bearing these words: "The Invisible Empire," "White Supremacy," "Pure Womanhood," "Dallas Must Be Clean," "Our Little Girls Must Be Protected," "All Native Born," "The Guilty Must Pay." They rode and marched through the streets silently and without interference from the authorities. Announcements of the purposes and objects of the Klan had previously been accepted and printed by the Dallas papers.

May 21, 1921.— At Sour Lake, Texas, Joe J. Devere, a justice of the peace, was tarred and feathered

May 23, 1921.— Ku Klux Klan paid $10 fine in police court at Dallas, Texas, for tacking signs on telegraph poles.

May 23, 1921.— At Dallas, Texas, John Moore, white, was seized in his home by masked men, taken to the outskirts of the city, stripped of his clothing and lashed with a horsewhip. He was accused of attacking a twelve-year-old girl. He fled town.

May 23, 1921.— At Houston, Texas, Ira McKeown, taxi driver, was beaten.

May 24, 1921.— At Dallas, Texas, John Parks was flogged by masked men.

May 25, 1921.— Jack Morgan, of Shreveport, was tarred and feathered by masked men.

June 8, 1921.— Dr. R. H. Lenert, at Brenham, Texas, was whipped, tarred, and feathered by eight masked men. He was charged with "disloyalty during the war" and with "speaking German."

June 8, 1921.— At Waco, Texas, K. Cummings was taken from his home by masked men, but escaped from his abductors.

June 8, 1921.— At Sea Breeze, Fla., Thomas L. Reynolds, a New Yorker, was assaulted while in his hotel by masked men, and beaten and shot.

June 13, 1921.— At Dallas, Texas, Edward Engers, filling station proprietor, was flogged by masked men and ordered out of town.

June 14, 1921.— At Houston, Texas, J. W. Boyd, a lawyer, was taken from his office by masked men and whipped. He was charged with annoying young girls.

June 17, 1921.— At Belton, Texas, James Collins, a negro, was given sixty lashes by masked men, and a placard, "Whipped by Ku Klux Klan," placed on his back, following his release from jail after a Grand Jury had failed to indict him on the charge of making insulting approaches to white women.

June 18, 1921.— At Goose Creek, Texas, E. L. Bloodworth and Olan Jones, oil field workers, were whipped, tarred and feathered by masked men, who charged their victims with being "undesirable citizens."

June 20, 1921.— At Goose Creek, Texas, W. Stewart, a jitney driver, was whipped, tarred, and feathered by twelve men after three passengers had lured him to a lonely spot. He was then ordered to leave town.

June 25, 1921.— At West Columbia, Texas, an unknown man was tarred and feathered and ordered to leave town.

June 21, 1921.— At Wharton, Texas, Henry Schultz was whipped, tarred and feathered after being kidnapped by masked men.

June 26, 1921.— At Yoakum, Texas, a white man, name withheld, citizen of the place for twenty years, was found on a lonely road, tarred, feathered and blindfolded.

June 27, 1921.— At Austin, Texas, Ku Klux Klan placards were posted warning against violation of moral codes.

July 1, 1921.— At Fort Worth, Texas, a white man whose name was not printed was taken from his home at 9 P.M. and given twenty lashes for alleged mistreatment of his wife.

July 4, 1921.— At Austin, Texas, Governor Neff, chief executive of the State in an address before the Rotary Club said that a crime wave had struck the State and that "the entire administration of the criminal code had broken down." On the same day warnings of the Ku Klux Klan were posted on the State Capitol grounds.

July 5, 1921.— At Fort Worth, Texas, Benny Pinto was

tarred and feathered and ordered out of town. A woman found with him in his automobile was taken home by his abductors.

July 8, 1921.— At Glidden, Texas, Harry Adams, a gardener, was beaten and choked by masked armed men. Then found to be the wrong man, he was released.

July 12, 1921.— At Enid, Okla., Walter Billings, a motion-picture operator, was given a coating of cotton and crude oil, after being whipped by masked men.

July 14, 1921.— One hundred masked men gathered at the jail at Greeneville, Texas, and unsuccessfully attempted to lynch Matt Olizen, negro, charged with killing Orbie Standlee.

July 14, 1921.— A delegation from Duncanville, Texas, warned the Dallas authorities that if Archie Holsome, charged with attacking a white woman was released, he would be lynched.

July 16, 1921.— At Tenaha, Texas, Mrs. Beulah Johnson, a white woman, was seized from the porch of a hotel, taken to the woods, stripped of her clothing, tarred and feathered preceding which her hair was clipped. Masked men wearing white uniforms attacked her, the woman said. They drove up to the hotel in three automobiles. Mrs. Johnson had been arrested on a charge of bigamy at Center, Texas, and was out on bond when she was seized.

July 17, 1921.— At Nacogdoches, Texas, J. M. McKnight was beaten by masked men.

July 17, 1921.— At Miami, Fla. At the close of his evening services, eight masked men waylaid the Rev. Philip S. Irwin, archdeacon of the English Episcopal Church, and head of the work of that church among South Florida negroes, carried him into the woods, whipped him, and then applied a coat of tar and feathers to his body. He was placed in a sack and taken in an automobile to a spot in the center of the town and dumped into the street. The following Tuesday, in response to a telegram from Rev. R. T. Phillips, rector of Trinity

Church, Right Reverend Cameron Mann, Bishop of Southern Florida reached Miami and conferred with several officials, also appearing before the Grand Jury in order to make a statement as to Archdeacon Irwin's work. In his report to the Presiding Bishop of the Protestant Episcopal Church of the United States, Bishop Mann said:

"About the middle of the afternoon, while I was consulting with the mayor and the circuit judge, the commander of the local post of the American Legion came in and stated that he had reliable information that if Archdeacon Irwin remained in the city he would be lynched, and that in all probability church property would be burned and numerous lives lost. He therefore asked that Archdeacon Irwin should agree to leave the city that afternoon."

The charge made by the mob against the clergyman was that he had preached "race equality" and "intermarriage." Bishop Mann declares unequivocally that Archdeacon Irwin does not hold to social or political equality for negroes in the United States, has never taught it, and in his missionary work has incurred disfavor with some negroes by his opposition to societies and movements which upheld the doctrine.

It was reported in the papers that the judge who brought the case to the attention of the Grand Jury told that body that, while the right of free speech is guaranteed, strangers should not defy the sentiments and traditions of the public.

July 16, 1921.— At Bay City, Tex., W. M. Hoopengarner, a banker, was tarred and feathered and beaten. The reason alleged was domestic infidelity.

July 18, 1921.— G. C. Benson beaten at Dickinson, Tex.

July 18, 1921. E. H. Peters, of Athens, Tex., was dragged from his room, beaten, dumped out of an automobile and seriously hurt.

July 19, 1921.— At Tenaha, Tex., J. W. McKnight was seized a second time by masked men.

July 19, 1921.— Declaring that he had information that fifty per cent of the members of the Oklahoma City police department belonged to the Ku Klux Klan, Mayor John C. Welton directed Chief Glitsch to investigate and to discharge every police officer who did not resign immediately from the Klan. On July 24, Mayor Welton was called on the telephone, and was told: "We warn you to lay off the Ku Klux Klan, or we will have to wait on you." The mayor paid no attention to the warning.

July 22, 1921.— At Hillsboro, Tex., a note from the Ku Klux Klan was received and published in the local paper as a "warning to some married men who should spend more time with their own wives."

July 26, 1921.— At Topeka, Kan., a warning was sent to Senator Capper's newspaper to "leave the Ku Klux Klan alone."

July 29, 1921.—Ben Wiley, of Lufkin, Tex., was put into a sack and tarred and feathered.

In the State of Missouri, a farmer aged sixty-eight years, was taken from his bed at night, removed out of doors and severely beaten by masked men; and a woman in Birmingham, Ala., was also maltreated by a mob composed of the same sort of individuals.

In most cases local sentiment appears to have been strongly with the perpetrators of the outrages, this being especially true at Waco, Tex. A man was assaulted by masked men at that place, but the victim succeeded in escaping from his attackers, recognizing three of the men who had seized him. He had them arrested, and they were bound over to await the session of the Grand Jury. Five preachers and the President of a Texas University signed the bonds of the men accused of mob violence.

In some parts of Texas, however, the depreda-

tions of masked individuals brought into being
a counter movement, and the *Dallas News*
notes the receipt of the following anonymous
communication:

"To the citizens of North Texas and the Ku Klux Klan:
"The Anti-Ku Klux Klan of North Texas announces
its being in the form of a mob.

"We intend and will do no violence unless the Ku
Klux Klan shows violence. We are in being and in force.
If necessary we will travel in force to do business in the
form of open warfare.

"The law will have its chance to show that we have
laws against mobs, white-capping, and acts of violence.
But we warn that being in Rome we do as the Romans do.

"We are unknown and unknowable. We will remain
that way. We hope that we will not have to resort to
populating lamp posts and using cold steel, but if so,
Oakland and Greenwood will boast of much activity and
the price of black crepe will rise. 'Anti-Ku Klux Klan
of North Texas.' "

A similar organization was announced from
southeast Texas. In an Associated Press dis-
patch from Beaumont, under date of July 27,
1921, it was reported:

"Organization is said to have been effected of a band
of men to combat the alleged activities of the Ku Klux
Klan, in South East Texas, with the announced intention
of conducting open warfare against the members of the
Klan if necessary 'because officers have not the nerve or
desire to place under arrest its members who have violated
the law.'

"First announcement of the new organization was set
forth yesterday in a communication addressed to the
Ku Klux Klan and sent to a local newspaper for publication. 'Squads of special service men,' the notice stated,

'have been appointed to locate members of the Klan.' It added that summary punishment would be inflicted upon any who are found. The communication said in part:

" 'We have formed a club, or mob, you may call it, of more than one hundred fearless men and we are going to stop you people with hot lead and hot steel at the first opportunity, and that will not be far off. We have sworn vengeance on such people and will shoot down like a mad dog men whom we learn to be members of the Klan.' "

Some of the newspapers of Texas have fearlessly taken a stand against the widespread epidemic of masked violence, even going so far as to charge them directly to the Ku Klux Klan. Notable among these has been the *Houston Chronicle*. In an editorial printed in August, 1921, under the heading "Law, or Secret Cult," it said:

"Once more the nation comes to a parting of the ways.

"The issue is clearly defined. No one but the unimaginative can misunderstand it.

"Constituted authority must prevail, or we are in for a reign of masked and irresponsible terror.

"The fine phrases with which apologies for the Ku Klux Klan defend it fall flat before what happened to that woman in Tanaha and that other woman in Birmingham.

" 'Law-abiding citizens have nothing to fear,' they declare, but what does that amount to when any citizen can be accused, seized and violently used without a hearing?

"Why do we bother about trial by jury, if the evidence of an angry and impulsive mob is sufficient to convict?

"Why have we built up a complicated system of justice, except to protect indicted citizens?

" 'Those eyes that see everything' and 'those ears that hear everything' have evidently missed the Magna Charta, the Bill of Rights, the Declaration of Independence and the Constitution of the United States.

"Once more they would thrust us back on the evidence of passion, and conviction by emotion.

"Once more they would rob the defendant of his right to be heard, to summons witnesses, to appeal to an impartial tribunal.

"Once more they would have punishment decided upon and inflicted by a council that cannot be held accountable.

"Once more they would expose everybody; whether criminal or not, to disguised tyranny.

"And they call it Americanism — this semi-barbaric horseplay that gives its victim no chance, that comes upon him unawares, that shuts his mouth and overpowers him by force.

"Innocent, or guilty, he has no privilege but to accept the inevitable, and that is what they call loyalty to their country and their country's institutions.

"Two women have been stripped and flogged, and this they say was done in the name of chivalry.

"Their names are written on a secret roster and their faces are covered, and this they assert is in keeping with those traditions of frankness, candor and open dealing which have been essentially characteristic of the United States.

" 'Those eyes that see everything' and 'those ears that hear everything' are evidently blind and deaf to the great struggle and dearly bought experiences by which Anglo-Saxon civilization has struggled from a state of tribal law to organized justice.

"A law that cannot be written is not fit to enforce. A charge that cannot be proved in an open manner is not fit to be made the basis of punishment.

"Persons who will not make accusations in the daylight are not fit to be believed.

"A theory of justice that does not afford the accused any time or right of defense is not fit to be defended.

"We are face to face with a mad conception of government, with an impossible basis of law enforcement.

"There can be no compromise with it, no half-hearted attitude. Either this idea of a secret cult purveying the morals of the people must go, or the sovereignty of the State will cease to exist.

"When a legislator defends the 'Invisible Empire' his allegiance is manfully divided. He is serving two masters — one of them created by the people, the other by a class within the people.

"True loyalty permits of no such divided allegiance, true patriotism recognizes but one master. Unless the overthrow of this government is intended, there is no place or excuse for the 'Invisible Empire.' "

CHAPTER XIV

Simmons Forced to Act

The cases of lawlessness set forth in the foregoing chapter have been laid at the door of the "Invisible Empire," but "Emperor" Simmons has denied that the acts involved were committed by members of his organization. There have been, however, three specific cases where outrages have been *proven* to have been committed by members of the "Invisible Empire," and in these cases the "Emperor" has been forced to take action against his own Klans, revoking charters in two instances and suspending the charter of the third. This action on the part of the "Emperor" has been extensively advertised by him as a guarantee of good faith that he intends to keep his "Invisible Empire" free from the control of lawless characters; but, public opinion, in the shape of widespread editorial comment of leading newspapers, does not agree with his point of view. Editors agree that no matter how altruistic may be the claims of the "Invisible Empire," a movement of secret government, acting extra-legally cannot be held in control; and it having been demonstrated in three specific instances that the Ku Klux Klan has been guilty of lawlessness, thus necessitating the "Emperor's" summary action, it follows that the whole system has no place in American affairs.

Believing that these developments in the Ku Klux situation fully sustain my position that the "Invisible Empire" is not a fraternal order, but a combination seeking to govern the American people by intimidation and force, I shall take up these cases in detail, the facts in each instance having been fully verified by the *New York World* in its investigations.

The first instance of lawlessness developed in Mobile, Ala., when people of that city awoke one morning in the spring of 1921, to find Ku Klux warnings on many billboards, trees, and telephone poles, and in other public places. Most of them laughed, but some of the negroes took the signs seriously and prepared to leave the city. A Northern exodus was threatened, but with all the excitement the newspapers of the city remained silent, not even printing the notice found stuck up about the place, although a New Orleans paper carried the story which was read by the negroes of Mobile. Fearing the action of public opinion, "Emperor" Simmons revoked the charter of the Mobile Klan.

The warning read:

"Law violators! This is the first and last time that we will warn you! You must either heed this warning or take the consequences, for if you have any doubts in your mind that you will not be able to comply with the laws of this city and county then you had better leave at once; 'for be ye well assured' that we will attend to you without fear or favor.

"This warning is for the taxi drivers, street smashers, bad women, shinny dealers, gamblers, thieves, loafers, and any and all violators of the law. We know you and have your names, and should you violate one of the laws after receiving this warning be ye assured that we will attend to you without hesitation, as the laws of this county must be complied with.

"No law-abiding citizens need fear anything from this organization for we stand back of the laws and see that they are enforced regardless. This is no negro whipping organization, but should occasion arise, be ye assured that we will not hesitate.

"This warning also applies to colored doctors. Seventy-two hours after this notice you must have the word 'colored' posted on your sign. This waiting on white patients must be stopped. We know you, and the next case that you attend don't blame us, as you have been warned.

"Bad women, you must obey the laws or then you must leave the city. This county shall be clean. Married men, you must look after your families and quit carousing; violation of this warning means unhealthy steps for you.

"We stand for the chastity of womanhood, peace and harmony in the home, law enforcement and protection of our homes and our families. Mobile County must be clean. Law violators, this means you.

"We are one hundred per cent Americans, and stand back of law enforcement, regardless.

"We do not fight anyone on account of their religious scruples nor will we tolerate same regardless.

"This warning is for those living in the jurisdiction of the Klan, and we are here twenty-five hundred strong to see that these warnings are carried out. Your next warning will be in person.

"(Signed) The Ku Klux Klan, Mobile City and County."

If the Mobile Klan really had twenty-five hundred members at the time its charter was revoked, it means that it had paid $25,000 into the coffers of the Ku Klux agents, to say nothing of some $16,000 paid to the Atlanta office for robes. It seems rather unkind of the "Emperor" not to have allowed the Mobile outfit something in return for its heavy outlay. Had it been permitted to continue, it could easily have beaten and tarred and feathered a few helpless women, driven out of town some of the taxi drivers and gamblers, and mutilated a few negro men. As it turned out, the Klansmen suddenly found themselves "all dressed up and no place to go," and in pretty much the same position as a lot of little boys who have been playing pirate and whose stern parents ordered them to come home.

The second instance of admitted lawlessness on the part of the national organization occurred at Pensacola, Fla., and was a particularly brazen attempt on the part of secret mob government to assume to enforce its own laws. About half past eight o'clock on the night of July 8, 1921, a delegation of the local Ku Klux Klan drove in automobiles up to the cafe of Chris Lochas, three cars loaded with Klansmen, wearing white robes and helmets, while other cars, similarly filled, stopped on the corner of the street. Three members of the Klan walked into the cafe and handed a letter in an envelope to Lochas. The message read:

"You are an undesirable citizen. You violate the Federal prohibition laws, the laws of decency, and you are a running sore on society.

"Several trains are leaving Pensacola daily. Take your choice, but don't take too much time.

"Sincerely in earnest."

When the letter was handed to Lochas, Captain Harper of the Police Department was standing inside the cafe, talking to the proprietor. Lochas opened the letter, looked at it and put it into his pocket, and thinking the matter a joke paid no attention to it. A few minutes later some negroes, who had seen the members of the Klan and recognized them for what they were, came into the cafe and their stories of the Klan caused Lochas to examine the letter more carefully and show it to the police. After delivering the message, the three members of the Klan walked out of the cafe, entered their automobiles and the three cars drove away into the night. The street was crowded at the time of the visit and hundreds of people saw the men in white robes halt their cars in front of the cafe and on the street corner, saw the messengers enter and leave the cafe and saw the cars drive away. In addition to the police captain who was on the inside of the cafe, a uniformed policeman was on duty immediately outside the door, yet neither the police nor any person present noted the license numbers of the cars or made any attempt to interfere with the visitors.

The *Pensacola News* in an editorial printed
July 9, 1921, said:

"Good citizens expressed themselves freely today concerning the occurrence of last night and were unanimous
in the opinion that in a community where the courts
are open and where the law is enforced by officers chosen
by the people, there is not the slightest justification or
excuse for any oath-bound secret organization, setting
itself up above the law and usurping the functions of the
duly constituted officers of the Government, meeting in
out-of-the-way places, acting in secret, and moving in
disguise, setting up its own standards of right and wrong,
acting as accuser, witness, judge and executioner, and that
the activities of such an organization will not be tolerated
in this community even if it should become necessary to
appeal to Federal authorities and invoke the aid of the
Government secret service men to arrest its activities.

"The opinion was freely expressed that if one body of
men acting in secret can command a resident to leave the
city under a veiled threat of personal injury, because
the organization conceives the idea that the man is
violating the prohibition law, another secret organization
of men has an equal right to invite a young woman to
leave town because perchance she might go in bathing
in a bath costume not in accordance with the views of
that organization; and another secret organization of
men might call an employer to his door at midnight and
give him a warning that he must raise the wages of his
employees or grant them shorter working hours, or suffer
personal violence.

"The activities of last night have been reported to
United States, State, and county officials, who are considering what steps to take in the matter. It is made a
criminal offense by city ordinance for any persons to
appear in public in disguise, and police officers have been
instructed to arrest any person appearing in public in
disguise. It is made a crime against the United States for
two or more persons to conspire against another to deprive

him of his civil rights, and it is made a criminal offense by the laws of the State for two or more persons to conspire or confederate to commit a breach of peace, and the State laws prohibit a rout, which is defined to be the assembling of three or more persons for any unlawful purpose. It is believed that the laws of the United States, the State and the city are ample to arrest the activities of any secret organization of the character mentioned."

As a result of indignation of the best citizens of Pensacola, Simmons suspended the charter of the Pensacola Klan, and offered to aid in discovering the perpetrators of the lawlessness, issuing a long statement which appeared on the front page of the Pensacola morning paper July 14, 1921, wherein he stated, with his usual sanctimonious whine that his organization stood for "the supremacy of pure Americanism without fear and without reproach," and gave expression, in his usual bad English, to his usual platitudes.

The *Pensacola News* in an editorial the same day challenged the "Emperor" to aid the authorities in detecting the criminals by giving the names of the members of the local Klan so they could be called before the Grand Jury and be examined under oath, and the names of the guilty parties thereby ascertained. The *News* further said:

" 'Pure Americanism' stands for equal opportunity, unabridged freedom within the law, orderly government, and the enforcement of the laws by the processes ordained by the Constitution. The anonymous communication, the ganging together of many to attack one, the affecting of a disguise, and the secret organization of men who took the law into their own hands in Pensacola on last Friday night, are the methods of the black hand, the mafia, and the nihilists. These organizations had their origin in Europe and cannot flourish upon American soil.

"There is no room beneath the Stars and Stripes for anarchy and bolshevism, for any organization that cannot afford to give the prosecuting attorneys of the Federal and State government the names of its members. The secrets of the organization will not be pried into, but the criminals will be handed over to the State for prosecution in the manner provided for by law.

"We repeat, the situation in Pensacola affords the K. K. K. and its Imperial Wizard an opportunity to show that their organization does not stand for lawlessness, that its members are law abiding, and that the organization will not countenance crime or its concealment by its members."

Simmons, of course, has never complied with this challenge, as far as has been reported in the newspapers, and it is doubtful if he ever will. He has issued a long-winded, verbose statement since that time rehashing the same platitudes that have characterized all his writings and speeches, but has not turned over to the authorities the names of his local members. The charter of the Pensacola Klan has merely been suspended, although the offense committed was far more flagrant and specific than the case of the Mobile Klan, and it is quite likely that should the matter "blow over" the Pensacola organization will be reinstated.

The third case in which the "Emperor" found it necessary to take public action against one of his Klans which had gone too far in pub-

licly advertising the "noble cause" occurred in
Beaumont, Tex., and attracted newspaper
attention on a nation-wide scale in the month
of July, 1921. It was the first time that a
Klan openly and publicly admitted its partici-
pation in an overt act of lawlessness. The case
was so brazen that the "Emperor" revoked
the Klan's charter.

It appears from an examination of the facts
in the case that masked men entered the office
of one Dr. J. S. Paul, in the city of Beaumont,
on the night of May 7, 1921, forced the physician to accompany them to a waiting automobile, conveyed him to the country, whipped him,
tarred and feathered him and ordered him to
leave town. A short time after that, similar
treatment was meted out to one R. F. Scott,
described in the dispatches as a veteran of the
Marine Corps. Much excitement prevailed in
Beaumont, until on July 21, 1921, a communication was received by the local newspapers under
seal of "Klan No. 7, Knights of the Ku Klux
Klan," of Beaumont, accompanied by a long
statement of alleged facts in the cases of the
two men who had been beaten.

Frankly admitting that its members had
attacked Paul and Scott, the statement went
into details as to the characters and conduct
of the two men. It was charged that Paul had,
for a long time, been making a business of
criminal operations on women, of the sale of
drugs and whiskey, and had waxed fat and

powerful in this alleged illicit business. It was charged that for the past five years repeated attempts had been made to have him indicted and convicted, but that on account of wealth and political influence, he had succeeded in evading the law. The climax of his alleged practices was reached in the case of a young woman, her name was not given in the statement, who was brought to Paul for an alleged operation. It appears from the charges made by the Klan that Scott was involved in the matter. According to the statements of the Klan, an operation was performed, from the results of which the woman was caused to suffer severe consequences, it being claimed that death nearly resulted from her condition. It appears further from the allegations that the woman called to see Doctor Paul and demanded financial assistance, asking for $1000 to reimburse her for her expenses incurred during her illness. This, according to the statement, Paul refused to pay, offering instead $500, which was refused, after which the woman was said to have been ordered out of the office. The rest of the story, told in the exact words of the Klan reads:

"Following this visit to Doctor Paul the girl visited the county attorney and related her story to him, but she pleaded that her father and mother be spared the shame of parading her misfortune to the world. She was assured by the county attorney that he was powerless to act unless she herself would file the complaint and testify against Doctor Paul. This she felt she could not do and left the court of law in despair. Then followed several days of unceasing agony the sufferings of the pangs of hunger and the remorselessness of a conscience that had been violated. The depths of despair were reached, suicide was the next logical step. The anguish-laden cry of that poor girl was heard by men who respect the great moral law more than the technicalities of the legal code. The heavy hand of the Ku Klux was laid upon Doctor Paul.

"For while the rabble with their thumb-worn creeds,
    Their large professions and their little deeds,
    Mingles in selfish strife, Lo! freedom weeps,
    Wrong rules the land and waiting justice sleeps."
                                    (Ku Klux Ritual)

"The eyes of the unknown had seen and observed the wrong to be redressed. Doctor Paul stood convicted before God and man as the murderer of unborn babies, the despoiler of little children, the social leper who sells the life of a human being for a money consideration. His victim was a poor girl. Doctor Paul was wealthy. Between the two stood the majesty of the law, draped in the technicalities of changes of venue, mistrials, appeals, postponements, eminent counsel skilled in the esoteric art of protecting crime and interpreting laws involved in a mass of legal verbiage, the winding and unwinding of red tape, instead of the sinewy arm of justice, wielding the unerring sword. The law of the Klan is justice.

"Doctor Paul was approached in his office by three men on the night of May 7, and instructed to go with them. He was placed in a waiting automobile and escorted a few miles out of town. The judgment of the Klan was read to him and charges were related to him, none of which he would deny. In a cowardly, whimpering plea, he plead that others were as guilty as he. The lash was laid on his back and the tar and feathers applied to his body. He was then informed that it was the will of the Klan that he should leave the city within forty-eight hours. Upon the return of the party to Beaumont, Doctor Paul was discharged from an automobile at the inter-

section of two of the main streets of the city that he might
be a warning to all of his ilk that decent men and women
no longer wanted him in the community. Doctor Paul
complied with the instructions of the Klan that he leave
the city and returned for a few days to his former home
at Lufkin. During this time he was under the constant
surveillance of the Klan."

When Doctor Paul returned to Beaumont,
according to the statement, he was invited to
appear before the Grand Jury for the purpose
of testifying about his attackers, but upon
appearing before that body, he was confronted
with the girl in the case, who, it appears, for
some reason not mentioned in the statement,
had decided to make a public complaint against
Doctor Paul in the manner prescribed by law.
Why it was any more improper for the woman
to have testified before the Grand Jury in the
first place than in the second the Klan does not
mention, but, according to its explanation,
Doctor Paul was indicted on several counts,
along with Scott, the other man involved, and
was released on bail. Here follows some very
excellent Ku Klux humor:

"Doctor Paul immediately made bond and was released
from custody, Scott was later arrested and in a few days
made bond and released. Doctor Paul for many days, in
company with his hired henchman, openly paraded the
streets of the city armed to the teeth in open defiance of
the law."

Here is Ku Kluxism in all of its glory. "In
open defiance of the law," utterly repudiating
the Bill of Rights of both Federal and State

constitutions, which guarantee a man the right
of trial by jury, this organization had abducted
a citizen, tried him secretly, convicted him, and
punished him and then whines because its former
victim armed himself as a protection against
further mob violence. Regardless of any and
all of the allegations against Doctor Paul, the
assumption of any set of men to secretly handle
the law enforcement of a community is nothing
more or less than anarchy.

It is very interesting and illustrative of the
Ku Klux state of mind to study this remarkable
document, for which reason I am giving copious
extracts. It appears that efforts of all kinds
according to the Ku Klux, were made by Paul
and Scott to kill the case, and the Klan claims
that Scott was persistent in his efforts to induce
the woman in the affair to leave town. The
statement continues:

"Scott was warned that his conduct towards the girl
must cease and that he would be required to stand trial
at the appointed time. This warning served no purpose
to him and his annoyances to the girl continued. Then
Scott, who had been constantly watched by the Klan,
whose number is legion, and whose eye is all seeing and
whose methods of gathering information are not known
to the alien world, was apprehended and punished in
the same manner Doctor Paul had been dealt with.
He was taken to the woods and guarded until nightfall.
His captors during this time treated him with kindness
and consideration. They provided him with food and
fruit to eat and ice water to drink. During the day he
was questioned and admitted all the charges the Klan
had accused him of. The judgment of the Klan was that

he was to be given ten lashes across the bare back and
that he was to be tarred and feathered and brought to
Beaumont to deliver two messages, one to Doctor Paul
that he must comply with the decision of the Klan that
he should leave town, but that he must return for trial
at the proper time. The other message was to another
person that the Klan would not allow the technicalities
to cheat justice any further in this case."

The statement concludes by an attack on
Scott's army record, and the allegation that he
had served a prison sentence, adding:

"Yet he poses to the gullible public and sensational
newspapers as a patriot and a hero. All these things the
eyes of the unknown have seen and their ears have heard.
We cannot be deceived and justice will no longer be
mocked."

Immediately following the publication of
this frank statement, "Emperor" Simmons
revoked the charter of the Beaumont Klan, and
announced his intention of sending investigators
to Texas for the purpose of looking into the
various cases that had been reported where men
in disguise had taken the law into their own
hands. Up to the time that this was written,
however, no such investigations have been
made or attempted, so far as the public has
been informed through the press.

The American people should view with alarm
the propagation of any organization, the result
of which has been the establishment of *one* unit
which assumes to itself the secret regulation
of law enforcement. Yet, when one studies the
ritual and the oath of the Ku Klux Klan but

little blame can be attached to the men in Beaumont for obeying what seemed to them the teachings of the "Invisible Empire." They had sworn to "use any and all justifiable means and methods" and, taking the literal construction of the oath, they saw what appeared to them a bad condition existing in their community, which they proceeded to rectify. The prime responsibility for the Beaumont case rests upon William J. Simmons for having solicited men to take an obligation that is in itself a violation of the letter and spirit of the laws of this country. His action in revoking the charter was forced by the publicity given to the case, and by the frankness and openness of his followers in assuming the blame for their acts. Speaking in ordinary street parlance, the action of the "Emperor" was merely "passing the buck" to his own people who had been "caught with the goods." When men are given a dangerous explosive to play with, the blame for the explosion that follows should be placed upon the person or corporation that gave it to them.

CHAPTER XV

SUGGESTED LEGAL REMEDIES

THE task of ridding the United States of the "Invisible Empire" will not be an easy matter. The people are prone to wait until the horse has completely disappeared before they begin to look after the security of the barn door. Until public sentiment is thoroughly aroused over the dangerous possibilities of an "Invisible Empire," such as is now being developed, it is unlikely that even the first steps will be taken toward suppressing it. The idea is so foreign to all the established order in this country that people will be slow in realizing what it is all about. Appreciating this fact and knowing that I possessed but limited facilities for bringing the matter to public attention, I felt prompted to turn over to the *New York World* all the information I possessed, and have that great newspaper inaugurate a nation-wide investigation followed by a publicity campaign that would make the "Invisible Empire" visible.

Exposure of a system, however, marks but the first step in eliminating that system. Publicity must be followed up by official action aimed at the accomplishment of concrete results, for unless this is done, the public mind is soon

diverted from the subject, and the exposure
becomes merely a newspaper episode. In the
present instance, exposure of the "Invisible
Empire," without legal action, will have the
effect of advertising it without harming it
in the slightest degree — and swelling its ranks
with thousands of new recruits.

In my opinion, the authorities of this country
should use every available piece of legal machinery to stop the propaganda, and new laws
should be immediately enacted rendering it
impossible to promote such a scheme in this
country in the future. It must be remembered
that the men who have launched this proposition have built up a large organization, many
of the members of which are fanatics. The
promoters have already seen the possibilities
of the scheme as a business proposition; they
have the names of the present members, which
can be used again; they have a fully equipped
plant for future operations; and in the event
the Ku Klux scheme fails, they will probably
try another one along similar lines. The system
itself must be destroyed and prohibited from
further action, either in its present costume or
in any other. Several lines of action suggest
themselves, but they may be broadly classified
under the two heads: Federal and State. There
should be concurrent action on the part of these
two governments.

I believe that Congress should enact legislation directed specifically at organizations of the

character of the "Invisible Empire." It should be provided that all organizations, secret or open, engaged in promoting racial or religious discord, should be prevented from sending their literature through the mails. The statute should be broad enough to include any kind of organized attempt to stir up class hatred, and officials of all such organizations should be held to strict accountability for the accuracy of statements sent through the mails. Misrepresentation of facts as to national, state or local conditions should be the basis of Federal action in breaking up such organizations. In the exercise of a national police power, Congress should be able to give the Federal Government the right to act against the heads of organizations, as well as a few individuals. In the cases that have come to light where there has been acknowledged violation of law by local Klans, Simmons has side-stepped responsibility by revoking and suspending charters. If Congress will pass legislation declaring that national officers of secret organizations are responsible for acts of their subordinates, and are subject to indictment, an important step will be taken in the right direction.

Since the chief asset of the "Invisible Empire" is its secrecy, Congress should pass an act providing that all secret orders or societies using the United States mails or engaged in the business of interstate commerce — as the "Invisible Empire" undoubtedly is — should be required

to furnish the Government with a list of names
of their members. The list should be required
to be in duplicate, one copy to be placed on
file, for public inspection, in the office of the
local postmaster, while the other copy should
be placed on file in Washington. The Government should also have the right to inspect all
books of account, showing funds that have been
derived from members either by interstate
commerce or by the use of the United States
mails. This removal of secrecy would, to a considerable extent, lessen the danger of Ku
Kluxism as a political force, and requiring publicity as far as membership rosters is concerned
would materially aid in making the system
harmless. I am quite sure that a publicity
statute would not work any great hardship on
the existing standard fraternal orders for most
of them have a yearly printed roster for distribution.

Under the Bill of Rights and the Fourteenth
Amendment to the United States Constitution,
the Attorney-General of the United States can
maintain actions against the "Invisible Empire"
on account of its activities in Texas, and have
no doubt that an official investigation of alleged
outrages would show some interesting facts.
In order to make the matter effective, however,
the investigation must be gone into very carefully and all of the facts uncovered. In August,
1921, the United States District Attorney in
Chicago announced that he intended to investi-

gate the Ku Klux Klan. In a few days, according to newspaper reports, he stated that he had been shown the charter of incorporation and other literature of the organization, and that he could not discover anything upon which he could base legal action. The charter of the organization does not tell all the facts, as has been demonstrated in the preceding pages.

Concurrently with the action of the Federal Government, the States can do some valuable work in stamping out Ku Kluxism, and preventing both the present "Invisible Empire" and its future imitators from operating. The "Invisible Empire" is known legally as the "Knights of the Ku Klux Klan, Inc." and was incorporated under the laws of the State of Georgia. So far as has been published in the newspapers, the only State in the Union where it has been granted a license to do business outside of its home state, has been in Indiana, where its charter was filed in August, 1921. In every State where it has not filed its charter and compiled with the corporation laws it has no legal standing whatever. Actions could be brought by the Attorneys-General of the various States restraining the Klan from further operation and also indictments might lie against the promoters for operating without compliance with the law.

As soon as it can be conveniently done, the legislatures of the States should enact various laws for the purpose of killing Ku Kluxism,

laws directed against membership corporations
stirring up religious and racial prejudice, against
secret membership, against unwarranted interference with the law-enforcing branches of the
Government, and against going about the
community in disguise.   More stringent laws
should also be enacted providing for the regis-
tration of foreign membership corporations seeking to do business from another State, especially
where money is taken from the public. If the
passage of "Blue-Sky" laws has had the effect
of protecting the public from being victimized
by all kinds of stock-selling schemes, surely
legislation could easily be enacted to carefully
scrutinize all alleged fraternal orders.

As to permitting foreign membership corporations to do business in a State, it should be
enacted that before being permitted to engage
in the business of soliciting members from whom
initiation fees or "donations" are to be secured,
the corporation should be required to file with
the Secretary of State a sworn statement of all
its national officers, its plans for doing business,
a copy of its charter of incorporation, its constitution and laws, and, where agents are employed
to canvas for members it should be specified
what compensation they are to be paid. These
agents should be licensed by the State as the
"Blue Laws" require the licensing of stock
salesmen. The organization should, furthermore, be required to file a bond with the Secretary of State insuring the good behavior of

the organization while engaged in business in the State, and it should be specified that the bond be forfeited should any local branch be guilty of committing a lawless act, in which case, also, the right of the corporation to do business in the State should automatically be terminated. No foreign corporation which permits its members to go about, in other States, disguised should be permitted to enter. After having complied with the foregoing provisions, the act should further provide that at stated intervals the secretary of each local branch be required to make two copies of the roster of membership of his branch, filing one copy with the county clerk of his county, and mailing one copy to the Secretary of State. These two copies should be open for public inspection at all times. In the event that the local branch fails or refuses to file its roster, the right of the national organization to do business in the State should automatically terminate.

As a matter of safeguard to the community, every State in the United States should have a statute enacted along the lines of the Tennessee Ku Klux act (Sections 6668, Shannons Code *et seq.*) which reads:

"6668. If any person or persons, masked or in disguise, shall prowl, or travel, or ride, or walk through the country or towns of this State, to the disturbance of the peace, or to the alarming of the citizens of any portion of this State, on conviction thereof (they) shall be fined not less than one hundred dollars nor more than five hundred dollars, and imprisoned in the county jail of the county wherein convicted, at the discretion of the jury trying the case.

"6669. If any person or persons, disguised or in mask, by day or by night, shall enter upon the premises of another, or demand entrance or admission into the house or inclosure of any citizen of this State, it shall be considered *prima facie* that his or her intention is to commit a felony, and such demand shall be deemed an assault with an intent to commit a felony, and the person or persons so offending, shall, upon conviction, be punished by imprisonment in the penitentiary not less than ten years nor more than twenty years.

"6670. If any person or persons, so prowling, traveling, riding, or walking through the towns or country of this State, masked or in disguise, shall or may assault another with a deadly weapon, he or they shall be deemed guilty of an assault with intent to commit murder in the first degree, and, on conviction thereof, shall suffer death by hanging; provided that the jury trying the case may substitute imprisonment in the penitentiary for a period of not less than ten years nor more than twenty-one years."

In connection with this Tennessee statute, it is interesting to note that the leading case, reported in the State, based on the act fully sustained the statute. In the case of Walpole against the State, 9 Baxter 369, delivered in 1878 by a Supreme Court composed entirely of Democrats, with several Confederate soldiers the court held:

"It is apparent that the object of this statute was to repress a great evil which arose in this country after the war, and which grew to be an offense of frequent occurrence, that of evil-minded and mischievous persons disguising themselves to terrify or to wrong those who happened to be the objects of their wrath or resentment. This was a kind of mob law, enforced sometimes by a multitude of vagabonds, who grew to be a great terror to the people and placed human life and property at the mercy of bad men, whose crimes could scarcely ever be punished because of the disguises under which they were perpetrated.

In closing its opinion the court said:

"The penalties of a violation of this law are severe, but they have proved themselves wholesome in the partial suppression already of one of the greatest of the disturbing elements of social order in this State. Affirm the judgment."

If every State in the Union will pass a law along similar lines to the above Tennessee statute, there will be no Ku Klux parades, no midnight burnings of the fiery cross, and no repetition of the tar and feathers occurrences that have been prevalent in the State of Texas. I think that there should be a modification, however, of the Tennessee statute, making it a misdemeanor to go about disguised in the daytime, and a felony at night.

There are already enough laws on the statute books of the States against mob violence, assault, murder, mayhem and other crimes, and the enforcement of these laws will go a long way toward killing the "masked terror." No law, however, is enforceable unless public sentiment is behind it, and if the public officials, especially the sheriff's forces and the city police departments are filled with men sworn to

obey "unconditionally" the orders of the
"Invisible Empire" and to use "any and all
justifiable means and methods" in the
accomplishment of the Ku Klux program even
public sentiment can do but little. In this
connection, I want to call attention to an
editorial which appeared in the *Searchlight*,
the official organ of the Ku Klux Klan, under
date of July 23, 1921, which reads:

"It is sometimes amusing to note the ridiculous situa-
tions which ignorance oftentimes leads men, even of
more than average intelligence. For instance, it doubtless
is amusing to members of the Knights of the Ku Klux
Klan to hear a judge instruct a grand jury to probe that
organization because of its 'lawlessness and un-Ameri-
canism,' when they know that anywhere from a third to
one-half the members of the grand jury are members of
the K. K. K., and know that the good judge is all uncon-
sciously making an ass of himself by attempting to express
an opinion on a subject that he knows nothing about."

The attempt of the Ku Klux Klan to enlist
the police authorities in its organization and
bind them with its vicious oath is the most
serious count in the indictment against the
system. The potentialities are far-reaching, and
unless the organization is checked in that
direction, the consequences must necessarily
be grave. How the situation, in that respect
should be met, I leave to others.

The foregoing suggestions are merely intended
to set people to thinking, and from these ideas
may come better suggestions as to the proper
methods which should be pursued in checking

and eliminating the rising tide of Ku Kluxism. It should be carefully remembered, however, that the task of wiping out Ku Kluxism will not be an easy matter. The organization is headed by a shrewd individual who has already tasted the sweets of success. All the energy that desperation and cunning can devise will be used in resisting any effort that will be made to suppress the organization. Behind this individual are thousands of fanatics, who for one reason or another believe that this "noble cause" is the salvation of the country. While fully one-half of the men who have parted with ten dollars went into the organization out of curiosity, and will probably drop it, the other element will do all it can to keep the movement alive, even in spite of the exposure made by the *New York World*.

Behind the publicity of the *World* should therefore come the united efforts of every agency in America which discountenances such a scheme. Every organization engaged in civic work should bring all the available pressure to bear upon the legislative branches of both State and Federal governments to secure the enactment of suitable laws against Ku Kluxism. Then when adequate laws are secured, the power of public opinion should demand that these laws be enforced and irresponsible and secret government, private regulation of the public peace, interference with law-enforcing authorities, and class hatred and prejudice should be crushed.

Half-hearted measures will do no good. Unless the American people are prepared to deal vigorously with Ku Kluxism, they may as well turn over to the system the free and untrammelled right to carry out its secret program, because mild measures will have but little effect in stemming the tide this movement must inevitably bring should its propaganda be successful.

CHAPTER XVI

THE *World's* EXPOSURE

I TURNED over to the *New York World* early
in July, 1921, the facts and documentary
evidence I had in my possession, and initiated
the exposure with the understanding that the
paper would make a complete investigation
before printing a single story. Under the
direction of Mr. Herbert Bayard Swope, the
Executive Editor and Mr. William Preston
Beazell, Assistant Managing Editor, the investigation was immediately begun. Mr. Rowland
Thomas was assigned to handle the investigation and direct the efforts of the force which
began working on it. This work was done for
two months, during which time I acted as an
assistant to Mr. Thomas.

On September 6, 1921, the *World* began the
publication of its series exposing the Ku Klux
Klan. Associated with the *World* were thirty
other newspapers covering practically the entire
United States, and for twenty-one days the
exposure of Ku Kluxism held over five million
newspaper readers spellbound in their absorbing
interest in the story of the organization. The
series comprised twenty-one articles, and occupied the front page in the *World* to the exclusion

of every big piece of news of national or international importance.

The exposure covered in the main facts and documents which I submitted to the paper. It fully substantiated and vindicated the charges made by me in my letter of withdrawal that the organization was un-American, that it was being propagated by spreading religious and racial hatred, that it was a money-making scheme for the benefit of a few insiders, that its oath was illegal and its ritual a sacrilege, and the various other matters referred to by me which are set forth in my letter in a previous chapter. With but few exceptions the entire American press agreed with my position in the matter by endorsing the *World's* exposure, and a vast number of the most prominent men and women in America publicly expressed themselves as gratified over the action of the *World* in showing up the Ku Klux Klan.

One of the most interesting developments made by the *World* in the course of its exposure was its publication of facts collected by the paper in connection with the relations of Edward Young Clarke, the Imperial Kleagle and head of the Southern Publicity Bureau, and his business associate Mrs. Elizabeth Tyler.

On Saturday, September 10, 1921, four days after the *World* commenced the publication of its series, Mrs. Tyler arrived in New York and engaged an elaborate suite of rooms in one of the most conspicuous hotels in the city.

She had obviously been sent by Clarke for the purpose of securing favorable publicity for the Klan, and immediately upon her arrival gave a story to an evening paper as "bait" for the Sunday papers. Although her mission was but a partial success, she did succeed in getting her picture in a few papers, together with prepared statements deploring the "unjust attacks" that had been made on the organization, and expounding its "noble aspirations." She was particularly emphatic on the proposition that one of the main objects of the Klan was to "protect the purity and chastity of womanhood and to preserve the sanctity of the American home." She stated that women were to be admitted to membership, that she had been made the first woman member, and that she would have charge of the women's department. While she was in New York "Emperor" Simmons issued one of his typically bombastic proclamations, composed in pure Simmonsese, designating Mrs. Tyler as his "Grand Chief of Staff." This proclamation read as follows:

"To all Genii, Grand Dragons and Hydras of Realms, Grand Goblins and Kleagles of Domains, Grand Titans and Furies of Provinces, Giants, Exalted Cyclops and Terrors of Cantons, and to all citizens of the Invisible Empire, Knights of the Ku Klux Klan, in the name of our valiant and venerated dead, I affectionately greet you:

"In view of our Nation's need and as an additional force in helping on the great work of conserving, protecting and making effective the great principles of our Anglo-Saxon civilization and American ideals and institutions, the Imperial Kloncilium, in regular session assembled, after deliberate care and earnest prayer, decided that there shall be established within the bounds and under the supreme authority and government of the Invisible Empire an organization that will admit the splendid women of our great national commonwealth, who are now citizens with us in directing the affairs of the Nation. Which decision of the Imperial Kloncilium I have officially ratified after serious, careful and devoted consideration of all matters and things involved by this move.

"In view of the foregoing, I hereby officially declare and proclaim that such organization does now exist in prospect. Plans, methods, ritualism and regulations of same are now in process of formation and will be perfected at an early date and officially announced.

"I do further proclaim that in order to have the proper assistance in the formation and perfecting of this organization, I have this day and date selected and officially appointed Mary Elizabeth Tyler of Atlanta, Fulton County, Ga., to be my Grand Chief of Staff, to have immediate charge of work pertaining to said woman's organization under my authority and direction.

"Further information will be duly and officially communicated from time to time.

"Done in the Aulic of His Majesty, Imperial Wizard, Emperor of the Invisible Empire, Knights of the Ku Klux Klan, in the Imperial City of Atlanta, Commonwealth of Georgia, United States of America, on this, the ninth day of the ninth month of the year of our Lord, 1921.

"Duly signed and sealed by His Majesty.

"WILLIAM JOSEPH SIMMONS,
                                            "Imperial Wizard."

Mrs. Tyler went back to Atlanta, complacently happy in the proud consciousness that she had "pulled" a wonderful piece of publicity. On Monday, September 19, 1921, however, the *World* and its associated newspapers printed a story that sent a shock of consternation into the hearts of the entire Ku Klux organization, stripped the mask from Mrs. Tyler and Clarke, and sent a ripple of merriment and disgust from one end of the country to another.

The story, which has been fully verified by the *New York World*, read as follows:

(*Special Despatch to The World from a Staff Correspondent.*)

"ATLANTA, September 18.— The *World's* exposure of Ku Klux took an astounding turn here yesterday when a staff correspondent obtained evidence of the truth of rumors which have long been matters of gossip in Atlanta. This evidence proves that:

"1. A few days prior to October 31, 1919, Edward Young Clarke of Atlanta, who is at present, by appointment of Imperial Wizard Simmons, the Imperial Kleagle or boss organizer of the Ku Klux Klan, and Mrs. Elizabeth Tyler of Atlanta, who recently, also by appointment and proclamation of Imperial Wizard Simmons, was made Grand Chief of the newly formed woman's division of Kluxters, were arrested at midnight and in their sleeping garments, in a notorious underworld resort at 185 South Pryor Street, Atlanta, run by Mrs. Tyler, and taken to the city prison, where Clarke was immediately placed in a cell and where Mrs. Tyler, after being searched, was also locked up.

"2. The two prisoners gave assumed names, as 'Jim Slaton' and 'Mrs. Carroll,' respectively, and being unable to obtain bail at that hour, were imprisoned until morning, when Francis Clarke, now managing and then city editor of an Atlanta newspaper and brother of Edward Young Clarke, now Imperial Kleagle of the Ku Klux Klan, appeared at the city prison and by giving $50 bonds effected the release of both prisoners.

Tried Under Real Names

"3. On October 31, 1919, 'Jim Slaton' and 'Mrs. Carroll' were brought into the Recorder's Court in Atlanta for trial on charges of disorderly conduct. After consultation with Policewoman Davis, who had participated in the raid and arrests, Recorder George E. Johnson ordered the prisoners docketed under their real names of Edward Young Clarke and Mrs. Elizabeth Tyler, and under those names they were tried, found guilty of disorderly conduct and sentenced to pay $5.00 fines or each work twelve days on the streets or other public works of Atlanta. They paid the fines.

"4. Additional charges of possessing whiskey, based on the finding and seizure of such liquor by the police in the Pryor Street resort at the time of the raid, stood against both Clarke and Mrs. Tyler, but were dismissed when J. Q. Jett of Atlanta, the son-in-law of the Mrs. Tyler who is feminine chief of the Ku Klux Klan, came into the Recorder's Court, claimed ownership of the seized whiskey and was fined $25 by the court.

"5. Clarke, Imperial Kleagle of the Ku Klux Klan, in its drive for $10 "one hundred per cent' Americans. consecrated and baptized to uphold and enforce the law and protect the sanctity of American homes and the chastity of American womanhood, at this moment stands on the public records of the Fulton County (Ga.) courts and the Atlanta City police courts as a man who has deserted and abandoned his wife and child and has not to this day denied these charges.

Testimony Given By Police

"Imperial Kleagle Clarke and Mrs. Tyler were arrested at midnight in their bedclothes in the resort, according to the testimony of the witnesses, Policeman Jameson, since dead, and Policewomen Davis and Voss, still on active duty. The resort was at 185 South Pryor Street, corner of Fair Street, and it was operated by Mrs. Tyler. The raid occurred a few days prior to October 31, 1919, which is the date of the hearing before Recorder Johnson, at which the verdicts of guilty were rendered and sentences imposed. The numbers of the cases of the City of Atlanta versus E. Y. Clarke and the City of Atlanta versus Mrs. Elizabeth Tyler on the Recorder's docket are 17,005 and 17,006, and the page number of the 1919 docket upon which they are listed is 305.

"Most surprising in view of Clarke's efforts then in progress to make America dry by collecting funds to help the Anti-Saloon League is the fact that the police found whiskey in the house and seized it.

"But next morning as stated the super-Prohibitionist and the Ku Klux feminist were absolved from the legal responsibility involved in the discovery of liquor on the premises when Jett claimed the whiskey and paid the fine of $25.

This story created one of the greatest sensations of the whole exposure, and was a blow to the entire propagation department. One Kleagle, A. B. Bate of New Jersey, wired to "Emperor" Simmons demanding the immediate removal of the offending pair. In reply to his telegram he was summarily dismissed as a Kleagle by Mrs. Tyler herself. For a few days chaos reigned in the Ku Klux Kamp. Clarke at first denied the truth of the story of his arrest, then made excuses, and then sent in his resignation to the "Emperor." Mrs. Tyler issued a statement branding Clarke as a "weak-kneed quitter," and repudiating him entirely. Simmons, knowing that the pair of professional publicity uplifters had made his organization declined to take any action against either of them, declaring that he had heard rumors of the story, but attached no credence to it.

Aside from showing up the records of a precious pair of "uplifters," the Clarke-Tyler episode has no great bearing upon the menace of Ku Kluxism. But the aftermath of the story's publication developed two sinister things that make necessary its introduction into this narrative. One of these was the printing in the *Searchlight* of a violent article which was practically a call to arms against the Catholics and others who were attacking the Klan. The other was the theft of the police records in the city of Atlanta, covering the cases against Clarke and Mrs. Tyler, obviously an inside job and showing the extent to which Ku Kluxism had control of the public officials of that city.

The incendiary article in the *Searchlight* from the pen of one Carl F. Hutcheson was headed "American Patriots, Hark!"

"American patriots! The womanhood of this country has been criminally assaulted in the most diabolical and satanic manner known to the human race — *an attempt* has been made to ruin the character of a good woman by the most dastardly methods of current times. That dastardly, cowardly and infamous instrument of murder comprises certain daily and powerful newspapers of this country!

"Murder! Yes, murder of the worst type! Those murderers who wield the pen, and strew infamy throughout every nook and corner of this nation by their millions of papers with their thunder-bolts of publicity against fair woman! Every word written in opposition to a great patriotic woman of Atlanta reeks with the blood of a grand innocent lady of Southern birth and standing. A woman's character destroyed (only temporarily), but that arch enemy of Americanism, the *New York World*, and its string of subsidized, patronizing, fawning and syncophantic sheets through America, commonly called 'newspapers,' but which are nothing more than organs, *and specialists as character assassins of the most despicable, contemptible and depraved sort!*

"The unwarranted murderous attack sprung from the brain of Pulitzer, who disgraces the name of his great father. His paper is located in a city and community where woman's virtue is played with, and her fair name is no higher regarded than a mere chattel lying upon a crockery-shop shelf for sale at a few pence. Had the so-called editor above referred to, and his blasphemous sheet, had any measure of fairness, justice, and just common canine decency, an effort to materialize effort in its opposition to the Knights of the Ku Klux Klan, he and his corps would never have focused their salacious and foul guns upon a lone, defenseless woman! I said alone? Defenseless? Not yet. By the eternal gods of justice, she is not alone and defenseless, as every mother's son of true Southern manhood and those of every other section of this country is aroused! We issue the bugle call to all of you to buckle on your armor, and defend this good lady, even with your lives!

"To you American patriots, we address ourselves! Unleash your dogs of war and make these hounds of convict stripe pay penalty for the great injury done. To you we appeal! Southern womanhood has been slaughtered! No woman's good name is safe from the glaring spotlight of a pernicious newspaper and its set of hirelings. Your mothers, sisters and daughters are unsafe from the millionaire newspaper owners, who prostitute their columns by crushing to death the fair name of a woman. They hesitate at no methods, regardless of how low in order, to carry out their designs as a means to their ends!

"Who is back of the damnable juggernaut which extinguishes a woman's life, character and reputation, in order to carry on the fight against the Knights of the Ku Klux Klan?

"Who is back of William Randolph Hearst's local paper, the *Atlanta Georgian*, which lifts from the *World* the false charges against our beloved woman, and defames her in her home?

"Whose tremendous influences, with their serpentine poison, inflames the negro of the North and East against the whites?

"Whose hands are seen beneath the cover of this murderous and slanderous propaganda?

"What manner of man was he who came into Atlanta for the *World* and wired back lies of the falsest and basest sort against an honest woman?

"By what license does a newspaper use its news columns to assert false charges as true?

"Who are the cowardly assassins in the background, who are pushing forward the fight against real Americans, by using weak-kneed Protestants and others?

"Who are the real murderers before and after the fact in the case of the fair woman murdered?

"Patriots, I take pleasure in tearing from their demoniacal faces, the masks!

"Patriots, *view the hellish countenances of Hundreds of Thousands of Knights of Columbus and millions of members of the Roman Catholic Church!* The latter despise real Americanism, hate our government, hate you, Patriots! They class your mothers, sisters and daughters as harlots, while the former is the monstrous iron wheel upon which the Roman Catholic Church hopes to crush America, American government, American institutions and purity of our women for the sake of the Dago on the Tiber — the hope of the Roman Catholic Church!

"Patriots, if ever red blood ran through your veins for pure American womanhood, innocent and undefiled Southern womanhood, for the purity of your home and household, let it run now with a warmth that knows no quenching! Yea, let your blood spurt fire!

"If there must be war with the Roman Catholics, the Knights of Columbus, and the hireling newspapers, editors and reporters, let it come! We are ready!"

The theft of the records from the police court occurred about ten days after the *World* had printed the Clarke-Tyler story. The representative of the paper, in getting the evidence of the arrest of the two persons had procured certified copies of the record, and had personally seen the original entries in the books. Upon going back again to look over the books, he found that all traces of the original record had been obliterated, the pages having been cut out and removed. The records were supposedly in the custody of the proper public officials who were responsible for their safety and their preservation from mutilation. No other organization aside from the Ku Klux Klan would have had the slightest interest in destroying the records.

CHAPTER XVII

THE KLAN BEFORE CONGRESS

CONGRESS was not in session when the *World* began the publication of its articles, and did not resume its sessions until the close of September, 1921. Many of the members of both houses were in Washington, however, and they followed the exposure of the Kluxes with close attention. Senators and Representatives expressed themselves as being gratified that the work was being carried on, and it became evident that when Congress resumed its session, there would be several resolutions introduced demanding an investigation of the Ku Klux organization. This proved to be true, and resolutions were introduced immediately after the two houses assembled by Representatives James A. Gallivan, of Massachusetts, Thomas J. Ryan of New York, Leonidas C. Dyer, of Missouri, and Peter F. Tague, of Massachusetts. As these resolutions were very much alike, the following, introduced by Representative Tague will be the only one reproduced:

"WHEREAS, There is being organized within the United States an anti-American organization known as the Ku Klux Klan, the objects and purposes of which are the exile and suppression of persons, members of certain races and religious sects, and

"WHEREAS, The accomplishment of such objects and purposes is in direct contravention of Articles I, XIII and XV of the Constitution of the United States, and

"WHEREAS, The organization known as the Ku Klux Klan has in more than one hundred instances been charged with unlawful seizure, abduction, trial and punishment of certain free citizens and residents of the United States, and

"WHEREAS, Such seizure, abduction, trial and punishment is a usurpation of legally constituted authority and in direct contravention of Articles IV, V and VI of the Constitution of the United States; therefore be it

"RESOLVED, That the Speaker of the House of Representatives be directed to appoint a special committee of five members of the House of Representatives, which committee is authorized and directed to proceed at once with an investigation of the organization, purposes and all matters connected with the Ku Klux Klan and to report its findings to the House of Representatives at the earliest practical day, together with such recommendations as it may see fit to make concerning the Ku Klux Klan, if any, and for this purpose the committee is authorized to send for persons, books and papers; to administer oaths; to employ a stenographer at a cost not exceeding $1.00 per printed page to report such hearings as may be had in connection with any subject which may be pending before said committee, the expenses thereof to be paid out of the contingent fund of the House of Representatives, and that said committee may sit during the sessions or recess of the House of Representatives."

All of the resolutions were referred to the Rules Committee of the House for the purpose of making a preliminary examination as to the advisability of appointing a special committee to investigate the Klan. This committee, of which Representative Philip P.

Campbell, of Kansas was Chairman, met on
Tuesday, November 11, 1921, for the purpose
of examining witnesses. "Emperor" Simmons
had been previously invited, and appeared
with counsel.

Rowland Thomas, appearing in behalf of the
New York World, was the first witness examined.
He placed before the committee the entire facts
that had been collected by the paper, showing
specifically that the Ku Klux organization
in some portions of the country had been guilty
of circulating anti-religious and anti-racial propaganda; that in some cases acts of violence
had been admitted by the local Klans; and
that the proposition was in all essentials a
money-making scheme. Covering every phase
of the system, Mr. Thomas concluded his statement as follows:

"We found also that they boasted or declared that
they were setting up an invisible empire here in the United
States. We found that their chief man had taken the
title of emperor and that he issued imperial and secret
decrees from an imperial palace. We found also, having
secured a copy of their oath, that every man who joined
this order pledged himself to obey without question all
the instructions of the emperor, who had been elected
for life. We found that severe penalties were threatened
to him if he failed ever in obedience. We found that part
of this oath was a pledge of impenetrable secrecy surrounding all the doings of the Klan. We found that each member
promised to keep at all costs, even that of life, in the face
of any coercion, persecution, or punishment, all secrets
of the Klan and all knowledge of the Klan committed
to him, with only four exceptions. He was not obliged

to keep to himself a violation of the oath of the Klan,
treason against the United States of America, malicious
murder, and rape. Those four secrets, apparently, he
could give up to other persons, three of them the crimes,
supposedly, he was at liberty to reveal to peace officers
and judicial officers of the United States Government.
All others, as far as the phraseology of the oath can be
read, he was to keep to himself. They belong to the Klan
and to the invisible empire and not to the United States
of America.

"We found them boasting that they had succeeded
in securing as members bound by this oath and made
citizens in this invisible empire many men who are also
officials of the visible, constituted Government of the
United States.

" 'Emperor' Simmons more than once made statements
that Members of the Congress of the United States —
both Representatives and Senators — belonged to his
invisible empire, and therefore were under his imperial
orders. He boasted that governors, mayors, and other
administrative officers, members of city councils, were
citizens of this invisible government, and that sheriffs,
policemen, police chiefs were citizens of the invisible
empire and that judges on the bench were members of it.

"The statement has been made publicly in print that
it amused a Klansman when he read in the press that a
judge had charged a grand jury to investigate the Klan,
because all Klansmen knew that a substantial part of the
membership of that grand jury would be Klansmen; that
the judge was a joke in making such a suggestion of
investigation."

C. Anderson Wright, who had formerly been
a King Kleagle, was also examined and verified
in many instances the facts that had been
presented by the *World*, although his testimony
in some respects lost its value by exaggeration
of financial estimates of the Imperial Palace.

He assisted, however, in verifying the fact
that the Atlanta organization had never undertaken any charitable or public work, and
appeared to be more of a financial scheme for
the benefit of the insiders of the movement.

Post-Office Inspector O. B. Williamson
furnished the committee facts and figures relating to the financial and business side of the
organization. Mr. Williamson had been to
Atlanta, talked with Clarke and Mrs. Tyler,
and had gone through the books of the Klan.
Among the first bubbles to burst was that of
the purchase of Simmons $25,000 home on
Atlanta's fashionable Peachtree Street. It
had been claimed by Simmons & Company that
this home had been presented the "Emperor"
by admiring members of the Klan, the money
constituting the purchase price having been
"donated" in small amounts ranging from
twenty-five cents to one dollar. According to
the real facts, Mr. Williamson showed the
arrangements for payments to have been as
follows:

"Ten thousand dollars was paid in cash, and one note
maturing October 15, 1921, was given for $15,500. The
deed was made in the name of E. Y. Clarke. The ten
thousand dollar cash payment consisted of $1000 secured
by subscription from Klansmen, $5000 from the Klan
treasury, and $5000 advanced by Clark and Mrs. Tyler."

It appeared from a statement of E. Y. Clarke,
quoted by Mr. Williamson, that this use of
Klan funds for private purposes was part of a

press-agent scheme to add to the dignity and apparently high standing of Simmons, as the latter was living in an unpretentious part of the city in a house not in keeping with his important position as "Emperor," and it was "therefore in the interest of the Klan to put him in a better home and one that would reflect credit on the organization."

Mr. Williamson also showed how Klan funds were diverted for private purposes in the purchase of Lanier University, introducing a statement of Clarke as follows:

"The Lanier University has existed for only a few years. It has been a Baptist institution of learning, operating under a charter granted by the State of Georgia and controlled by a board of trustees of fifteen men. Some time in July, this year, representatives of this university approached Colonel Simmons and myself with a proposition to purchase the university outright and assume, of course, its debts, which amounted to $50,000. We had our attorney to investigate the matter fully and we found the indebtedness much larger than claimed. We therefore rejected the proposition to purchase and submitted a counter proposition. The counter proposition was accepted and was in substance as follows: First, that the managing board elect Colonel Simmons president of the university. Second, that they agree to make it nonsectarian. Third, that the present existing board elect new trustees, as named by Colonel Simmons, the present board resigning in their favor.

"Now, following that is other information, the material part of which is that the Klan paid to this university $22,474.32, a part of which was out of the Klan treasury and which is not secured in any way."

Mr. Williamson testified that he had gone
over the books of the organization and had
found that while the financial records of the
organization had been accurately kept since
June 15, 1921, there had been no accurate
record kept prior to that time, embracing a
period of one year during which time the Klan
had been propagated under the contract of
E. Y. Clarke, printed in a previous chapter.
The gross receipts of the organization, according
to Mr. Williamson were $1,148,710.97; the
books showed 85,126 members; and statements
of Clarke placed the membership at 126,000.
The Post-Office Inspector stated that prior to
June 15, 1921, about $151,000 had been spent
by the organization, but that he had been
unable to secure any statement as to the manner
in which it had been disbursed. In utter dis-
proof of the claim that the organization had
been established for benevolent purposes, it is
interesting to follow a part of the testimony
of Mr. Williamson in detail:

"MR. CAMPBELL. The ritual of the order and the
proclamation hold out the order as one for benevolent
and high purposes?

"MR. WILLIAMSON. Yes, sir; and not for selfish profit.

"MR. CAMPBELL. What did you discover with respect
to the use of money for beneficial purposes to the
public?

"MR. WILLIAMSON. Well, when I went to Atlanta
I found that the imperial palace itself, which had been
bought in part with Klan funds, was in the name of Mr.
Clarke. I found that the home of Mr. Simmons, which
had been bought in part with Klan funds, was in Mr.

Clarke's name. I found also that some $21,000 of Klan
funds had been given the Lanier University without
security. And in that connection I might say this: That
whenever anybody pays his $10 for the purpose of joining
this Klan, he is given a receipt which says that this money
is received in trust for the Knights of the Ku Klux Klan
(Inc.). That is printed on each and every receipt.

"Mr. Campbell. What is the amount that has been
paid out for salaries of officers in Atlanta — out of the
money that has been collected, if you know?

"Mr. Williamson. Well, I can tell you that, from the
propagation department alone, $15,247 has been paid as
executive salaries.

"Mr. Campbell. To whom has that been paid?

"Mr. Williamson. Well, I take it, from the word
"executive," that it must be Mr. Clarke, and Mrs. Tyler,
because they are the two executives of that department.
Then the field men — they are the Kleagles — have
been paid, in round numbers, $464,000. That would
be $5 out of the $10, of which $4 would go to the Kleagle
and $1 would go to the King Kleagle. That uses up $5.
Then 50 cents goes to the Grand Goblin. And it is all
used up but $4.50 and $2 goes to the Klan.

"Mr. Campbell. And all of the $8, then, is used up
in paying officers or agents of the Klan?

"Mr. Williamson. That is true.

"Mr. Campbell. How much of the remaining $2
has been spent, if you know, for the benefit of needy
people, or for helpful purposes in communities — charitable purposes?

"Mr. Williamson. Well, if you call Mr. Simmons
a needy person, then some thousands of dollars have been
spent for him. But general charity, I do not think, has
received any of it; at least it does not appear on the
accounts.

"Mr. Campbell. What is Mr. Simmons' salary, if
you know?

"Mr. Williamson. Mr. Simmons at present gets

$1,000 a month. He has been getting that since the first of August."

When questioned as to the activities of Mrs. Elizabeth Tyler, Mr. Williamson described her as a business woman who was engaged in the work of propagating Ku Kluxism as she would in any other mercantile pursuit, without any altruistic motives whatever. This is brought out in the following colloquy:

"MR. CAMPBELL. It is purely a business proposition, so far as she is concerned?
"MR. WILLIAMSON. Absolutely.
"MR. CAMPBELL. She is using the mysticism, the regalia, the paraphernalia, the masks, and all of the literature of the order for the purpose of making money out of it? Is that correct?
"MR. WILLIAMSON. That is correct. In fact, she told me at least twice that she was in the business for the purpose of making money, just like she was in any other business for that same purpose."

William J. Burns, Director of the Bureau of Investigation of the Department of Justice, was called as a witness, but stated that his department was still investigating the Ku Klux Klan and that he had nothing to offer at the present time.

His Majesty William Joseph Simmons, "Emperor" of the "Invisible Empire," Knights of the Ku Klux Klan, was the last witness examined.

Having a good conception of the theatrical, he had arranged to be introduced to the com-

ᴸᵘittee by Congressman W. D. Upshaw, of
Georgia. In spite of the remark from Chairman
Campbell that Simmons did not need an introduction to the committee, the "Cracker" Congressman cleared his throat and delivered the
following "spread-eagle" speech:

"Knowing his sterling character, as I do, I am prepared
to underwrite his every utterance as the truth of an honest
patriotic man. I do not know "what all" Colonel Simmons
has been doing behind closed doors, but I do know that,
as a sturdy and inspiring personality, as a heroic veteran
of the Spanish-American War, as an honored Knight
Templar and member of something like a dozen other
honored and well-known fraternities, as a consecrated
churchman, and a God-fearing citizen, he is as incapable
of an unworthy, unpatriotic motive, word or deed, as
the chairman of this committee, the Speaker of the
House of Representatives, or the President of the United
States.

"I have known this good man to use his great influence
to stop an incipient race riot. I have known him to
dispense benevolence to a negro educational institution.
I have known him to prevent negroes from being mobbed
for crime, even as they were recently mobbed for no crime
by white men in Omaha, in Chicago, in Indiana and even
here in the Nation's capital.

"Not for one minute would I stand for personal or
organized wrongdoing by any man or any friend. More
than any other Congressman, because of my relationship
to this district, I want to know the light and I want the
world to know the light and I want the country to know
the light concerning this organization and other secret
organizations whose deeds are questioned by many and
whose memberships are limited by race, creed, or color.

"I have the privilege, gentlemen of the committee,
of presenting to you my long-time, personal friend and
constituent, Col. William Joseph Simmons."

Simmons, no doubt, expected great applause from the committee, but, instead, was met with the cold remark often used by the police authorities: "You are notified that whatever you may say will be used against you."

The "Emperor" was on the stand for three days and his testimony before the committee with its accompanying exhibits fill over a hundred printed pages of the record of the proceedings. Analyzing his statements, I should say that in many respects he was an excellent witness who verified completely the charges made against his organization by the *New York World* and myself.

Denouncing me for repudiating my oath of allegiance to his "Invisible Empire" by exposing its secrets, he proceeded to go much farther than I had done, by turning over to the committee his ritual, oath and many other documents to which I had never had access.

His testimony can be classed partly as confession and avoidance; partly as denial of facts that were clearly proven by the *World;* partly as attempted cheap wit that had no element of humor whatever in it; considerable denunciation of the *World* and of myself; many wild and erratic statements without foundation of fact; and a great deal of praise both for himself and for the organization he represented.

Among his denials, for example, he stated that Mrs. Elizabeth Tyler had no connection with the organization except as an assistant

of Clarke in his publicity work. This statement
was made in the face of the fact that less than
thirty days previously he had issued a "ukase"
making the Queen of South Pryor Street his
"Grand Chief of Staff." He denied that the
Klan at Beaumont, Tex., had perpetrated the
outrages against Doctor Paul, when it had been
proven under the official seal of that Klan that
it had maltreated Paul. He denied responsibility in the Pensacola and Mobile cases, in spite
of the fact that he had taken official action
himself. He denied that he had given the
interview to the *Searchlight* previously mentioned, in which he predicted direful things
would happen to the enemies of the Klan.
These are merely a few denials of previously
established facts, facts so well established that
any jury in the country would accept them.

He was particularly bitter against the *World*,
and lost no opportunity of denouncing it.
Included in some of his choicest attacks on the
paper were the following:

"The attacks against the Klan were originated and
started by the *New York World*, which is owned or controlled by a Jew, Mr. Pulitzer, whose main purpose is
circulation and revenue. The circulation manager of this
paper stated to one of the newspaper trade publications,
the editor and publisher of New York which publi hed
this statement, that the Ku Klux attacks had added a
hundred thousand circulation to the *World* and additional
advertising.

"The *World*, according to their own statement, spent
over four months, with unlimited resources at their
command, in an investigation of the Knights of the Ku

Klux Klan, using trained investigators, newspaper men, and covering every section of the country. In the face of this careful investigation the *World* has not been able to prove anything detrimental to the Klan except their own colored views of unfounded rumor and expressing the attitude of its Jewish ownership.

"The *World* saw that the Klan was the fastest growing purely Protestant, non-political organization in the United States. The *World* knew that when you strike at a man's religious and fraternal organizations you are striking at the very fiber of his being and that then all political affiliations and party lines are forgotten.

"The *World* is the stronghold of the Democratic newspapers and the Democratic Party, and it has been said by those in a position to know that if the *World* could, by shrewd propaganda and untruthful slanders, force a Republican Congress and administration to throttle or destroy a purely local American Protestant fraternal organization, as is the Ku Klux Klan, that its hundreds of thousands of members, friends, and those who think as does the Klan, would at the polls three years from now forget party lines and preference and vote the Democratic ticket.

"I wish to notify the chairman of this committee that there are plans on foot at the present time whereby one of the representatives of the *New York World* is to be tarred and feathered in the name of the Klan, and that this plan has been originated and its details worked out by representatives of the *New York World* so that it will appear that the Klan did this in a spirit of revenge. Furthermore, through this plan the *World* hopes to be able to secure additional circulation and advertising for their paper in keeping alive this matter. The congressional investigating committee that I want to investigate the Klan will receive the sworn proof of this plan of the representatives of the *World* to further try to discredit or harm the Klan."

These statements are fairly good examples of the misinformation and erratic statements the "Emperor" gave the committee. He probably did not know that Ralph Pulitzer is a communicant of St. Thomas Episcopal Church, and that the exposure of his political-financial scheme was no more Jewish in origin than Simmons is himself. That the circulation of the *World* increased 100,000 copies a day is the truth, but it was due to the fact that the American people wanted to find out the facts about Ku Kluxism, and it is significant that, in New York City, from which all this gain in circulation came, Ku Kluxism has been unable to make any progress since the exposure was made.

Among the exhibits presented by Simmons to the Rules Committee was his secret constitution, which up to that time had been a private document. This revealed the fact that Simmons has created for himself a life-time position at a good salary. The Constitution, Article 8, Section 2, reads:

"The Imperial Wizard shall hold office for life or during good behavior. He may be removed for just cause by an unanimous vote of the Imperial Kloncilium, or after charges have been preferred and a trial upon three-fourths vote of said body in session assembled."

This unusual section did not appear to the "Emperor" to be anything extraordinary, his comment being: "As long as the old horse is pulling well, it is no use to take him out of the

harness when you have him harnessed up. He
cannot do you any harm."

Simmons modestly stated to the committee
that he had no vision of turning the United
States into an Empire. He stated, among
other things:

"If tomorrow morning our great President Harding
should resign, and all the functioning faculties of our great
American Government would become instantly paralytic
and if the American people should rise up and proclaim
me the monarch of America, I would die before I would
accept it."

While modestly laying aside the Imperial
crown, Simmons, however, placed himself in
the distinguished company of Julius Caesar,
Jesus Christ and George Washington, as he gave
utterance to the following choice outburst:

"Julius Cæsar had his Brutus, Jesus Christ had his
Judas, and our great and illustrious Washington had his
Benedict Arnold. Sir, I can state to you that I can enter
the fellowship of all three of those because I have suffered
in my soul as a result of the treasonous and treacherous
conduct of traitors. I refer to one in the beginning of my
statement this morning. Right recently, those who have
furnished material to the outside world and whose names
have been put across the page, are one man by the name
of Craven, of North Carolina; another man by the name
of Fry, who hails from Tennessee; another man by the
name of Wright, who hails, so far as I know, from New
York. Mr. Craven was a disgruntled office seeker who
tried to have me appoint him as State head of the State
of North Carolina. When I had not made any appointments along that line, and had not gotten to that, I
understood he was trying to get the appointment to use
it for political purposes. The appointment was not made

at the time he wanted it, and he sent threatening letters, and because he did not get it, or because he could not get that appointment, he became a disgruntled office seeker in this Order and proved a traitor to his sacred trust. Mr. Fry, or Captain Fry, as he is called, was in our field force. He also proved a traitor, and violated as solemn an oath as a man can take."

Simmons admitted, in discussing his ritual that he had appropriated without any credit the immortal poem of Josiah G. Holland entitled "God Give Us Men," but made no effort to defend himself against the charge of plagiarism, frankly stating that he had taken the poem and but slightly paraphrased it.

The climax of Simmons testimony was a highly theatrical and emotional "break down," which some observers have declared to have been deliberately staged for the effect it produced, although Simmons claims that it was caused by an illness from which he was suffering at the time. After concluding his long-winded statements and verbose testimony he turned to the committee and cried:

"Again I want to express to you, Mr. Chairman, my deep gratitude and thanks for the courtesies you have extended to me. I want to say to all those men and women who have given assurance, with your permission, of their belief in me that they have my thanks, and I want to say to my persecutors and the persecutor of this organization in all honesty and sincerity no matter to what creed or race you may belong in your persecutions, through the medium of the press or otherwise, that you do not know what you are doing. You are ignorant of the principles as were those who were ignorant of the character and work of the Christ. I cannot better express myself than by saying to you who are persecutors of the Klan and myself, 'Father, forgive you, for you know not what you do,' and 'Father, forgive them, for they know not what they do.'

"Mr. Chairman, I am done."

He then fell forward, face downward on the table.

CHAPTER XVIII

CONCLUSION

THE facts which I have endeavored to set forth in these pages should have caused the reader to do some serious thinking, for serious thought is something this country at present needs above all else. The United States has but lately emerged from the greatest war in the annals of the race. When we laid down our arms the might and power of the German Emperor was forever crushed. Having assisted materially in crushing a visible Empire in Europe, the American people should be able to make short work of exterminating an "Invisible Empire" at home. When this righteous task is accomplished, they should pause a little and reflect upon some of the conditions that exist in this country today — conditions that must be soberly and earnestly faced.

There has never been a period in American history where sounder, saner, and more intelligent leadership was a prime necessity than it is at present. Totally unprepared in every way to enter a war on such stupendous a scale, American idealism and American practical sense were fully adequate to meet the abnormal situation; but the termination of the war found

the country still functioning abnormally. To
accomplish successfully the return to normal,
pre-war conditions has been, is, and will be the
chief thought of the leaders and the people.
Economic conditions require readjustment,
important matters of trade must be regulated,
vital questions of finance and taxation must be
handled, in fact, the whole country must settle
down to production, manufacture, distribution
of merchandise, and the transaction of the
nation's regular business.

These matters alone should be sufficient to
occupy the entire attention of the people, but,
unfortunately, there exists in the United States
a series of group antagonisms that bode no
good for the future peace and prosperity of the
country. The fact that there are a number
of discordant groups in America is the basic
reason why the Ku Klux propaganda has been
so successful. The further fact that the country
requires all of its best thought to the readjustment of its vital interests makes it all the more
dastardly to stir up domestic dissension in the
United States at this time of all others. These
group antagonisms are of such importance
to the country that until they become reconciled
and subordinated to the common public interest
there will never be, on this side of the Atlantic
Ocean, a cohesive, homogeneous nation such
as is the British Empire. The development of
a national unity for the United States, which
really began at the termination of the Civil

War, is yet in its infancy stage. Outwardly the nation is, to all intents and purposes, great power, rich, inventive and capable of meeting the most terrific forces that might be arrayed against it; inwardly, it is a collection of discordant elements, many of which assume the prerogative of dictating to the others. If the United States ever goes to pieces, the cause of its disintegration will not be due to foreign aggression but will result from internal strife.

The tendency of unwarranted dictation of one group to another has produced in recent years the voluntary "uplifter," who, generally for personal gain, has, with his followers, presumed to take charge of the personal habits, the morals and the liberties of the community under the alleged plea of elevating the community. This is one of the phases of the Ku Klux movement, which, surreptitiously, would attempt to pry into the affairs of the people of a community, and assume to itself the prerogative of regulating their private matters. It is, however, but a natural outcome of a general condition. I believe, however, as a general thing:

The American people are "fed up" on the "uplift!"

It would be a great blessing if ninety-nine per cent of all the associations and societies of the "uplifting" character were completely wiped out of existence, and the public be permitted to try the wholesome experiment of attending to

its own business without the assistance of
meddlesome individuals whose sole means of
livelihood consist in professional "uplifting."

Another situation in America that may be
classified as a group antagonism is the race
question which must be settled by practical
common-sense methods founded basically upon
the elementary principles of justice. For fifty
years the American negro has been the football
of party politics, and as a result both the negro
and the country at large have been sufferers.
When the negro ceases to be a political issue
and when the "uplifters" keep their hands off
of him and let him work out his own salvation,
he will become a better and more useful citizen.

Other group antagonisms that exist in America
are Capital and Labor, Radicalism, and religious
groups of all shades and varieties. In the matter
of Capitalism and Trades-unionism, the average
American is between Scylla and Charybdis,
and is inevitably the victim of both discordant
elements. The burdens of taxation, high prices,
and labor disputes fall upon the shoulders of
that vast army of Americans constituting the
middle class. Intruding its ugly head into the
industrial situation comes radicalism as a disturbing factor in unbalancing the peaceful conditions of the country. All these divergent
groups must be co-ordinated and taught a
national unity — a more profound respect for
real Americanism — before this country can
truthfully call itself a really great nation.

Perhaps the most senseless of all group antagonisms is the religious. It is a peculiar thing to the student of world religions to note the extraordinary amount of friction and discord that has attended organized Christianity almost from its inception, resulting oftentimes in persecution and bloodshed. It was, in a great measure, to escape the religious intolerance of Europe that many of the first settlers came to America. The Puritan, driven from England, sought the rock-bound shores of New England; the Quaker immigrated to Pennsylvania to found a colony, based upon the principle of brotherly love; the Catholic, led by Lord Baltimore found refuge in Maryland; the Cavalier settled Virginia; and, to the Carolinas came the Huguenots,— all seeking the privilege of worshipping God according to the dictates of personal conscience. So strong was the feeling against religious intolerance, and so jealous were the early fathers of the principle of religious liberty that the very first amendment incorporated into the Constitution of the United States read: "Congress shall make no law respecting an establishment of religion, or prohibiting the free exercise thereof."

For one hundred and twenty-five years, more or less, the antagonism of religious groups was not felt to any great extent, but in recent years there has been a steady increase of religious discord. There has been antagonism between the Christian and the Jew, between the Protestant and the Catholic, and between the various sects and denominations that profess and call themselves Christians.

The anti-Semitic feeling in the United States is due, in my opinion, to several causes. I think primarily it is based upon a feeling of jealousy of the Jew's great advance in America along all lines of commercial and professional activity. When one considers that there are only a little more than three millions of Jews in the United States, it is astounding what great progress they have made in practically every field of endeavor. The popular conception of the Jews as merely commercial people is not borne out by the facts, because in the legal, medical, and scientific professions, in music, in the drama, and in the arts some of the leaders in America are Jewish people. Instead of meeting this unusual rise by emulation and competition, many people give vent to their jealousy through the channels of an unreasoning anti-Semitism. On the other hand there is a great deal of legitimate criticism against the extremely lower classes of foreign Jews who have been permitted to come indiscriminately to American shores, people who are ignorant of real Americanism and unwilling to learn. The general characteristics of these people are eagerly seized upon by the professional Jew-baiter, and consequently the great mass of Americans of Jewish origin, men and women of refinement and ability are made the targets of a general attack of anti-Semitism.

There is a great deal more anti-Catholicism in America than the average person realizes, and the sooner the Protestants and the Catholics find some common ground of agreement, the better off this country will be. Much of this sort of group antagonism could be eliminated if both sides of the controversy would get together and abandon the spirit of intolerance that is characteristic of each. The increase of Catholicism in America has been very rapid. There are now over seventeen million Catholics in this country, and they are found to a great extent in the larger cities. In these places the church is a force for great good, controlling people that no other religious organization can control, and should its good influence suddenly be withdrawn, the most wretched conditions would prevail.

I do not believe that the Protestant churches possess the ability to cope with certain phases of metropolitan life as successfully as does the Catholic Church.

Basic causes of group antagonism between Protestant and Catholic lie partly in the fact that the government of the Catholic Church is outside of the United States, and partly on account of the attitude of the church itself toward certain American institutions, notably the public-school system and the laws in this country governing marriages. If the Catholic Church was under an American head, with no connection with any foreign organization, there would be but little ground upon which the professional Catholic-baiter could stand, but the fact that it is governed from Rome furnishes the chief objection to the system. In spite of this however, it lies in the power of Protestant and Catholic leaders to "get together" and endeavor to eliminate the present growing friction. In my study of the Ku Klux movement, I found that one of its greatest bids for popular favor was in its attitude to the rise of Catholicism in America. The fact that such a thing can be true, should be a matter of serious reflection to the Catholic and to the Protestant. In the succeeding years, if this feeling is not allayed and the differences reconciled it means mischief.

I believe in a real Americanism based on a deeply rooted love of country, and a broad respect and mutual understanding on the part of the people. I believe firmly that all of the internal dissensions and discords in this country, where group is arrayed against group could be completely eliminated by the application of the philosophy and love of Jesus Christ. "Invisible Empires," "Ku Klux Klans," and all organizations seeking to advance one group at the expense of another, pale into oblivion and nothingness, when the voice of the gentle Nazarene speaks down the centuries, breathing a sweet message of brotherhood alike to the white man and the negro, the Gentile and the Jew, the Catholic and the Protestant, giving to each the same message, and voicing a common creed:

"Thou shalt love the Lord thy God, with all thy heart, and with all thy soul, and with all thy strength, and with all thy mind, and thy neighbor as thyself.

"On these two commandments hang all the law and the prophets."